Let
Me
Count
the
Ways

Also by the authors

BY MARTY KLEIN, PH.D.

Your Sexual Secrets: When to Keep Them, When and How to Tell

Ask Me Anything: A Sex Therapist Answers the Most Important Questions for the '90s

BY RIKI ROBBINS, PH.D.

The Empowered Woman: How to Survive and Thrive in Today's Society

Negotiating Love: How Women and Men Can Resolve Their Differences

Betrayed! How to Restore Sexual Trust

Let Me Count the Ways

Discovering Great Sex Without Intercourse

Marty Klein, Ph.D., and Riki Robbins, Ph.D.

Jeremy P. Tarcher/Putnam • a member of Penguin Putnam Inc. New York

Most Tarcher/Putnam books are available at special quantity discounts
for bulk purchases for sales promotions, premiums, fund-raising,
and educational needs. Special books or book excerpts also
can be created to fit specific needs. For details, write
Putnam Special Markets, 375 Hudson Street, New York, NY 10014.

Jeremy P. Tarcher/Putnam
a member of
Penguin Putnam Inc.
375 Hudson Street
New York, NY 10014
www.penguinputnam.com

Library of Congress Cataloging-in-Publication Data

Klein, Marty.
Let me count the ways : discovering great sex without intercourse /
Marty Klein and Riki Robbins.
p. cm.
Includes bibliographical references.
ISBN 0-87477-956-1
1. Sex instruction. 2. Sex. 3. Sexual intercourse. 4. Sexual
deviation. I. Robbins, Riki. II. Title.
HQ31.K618 1998 98-42900 CIP
306.7—dc21

Printed in the United States of America

1 3 5 7 9 10 8 6 4 2

This book is printed on acid-free paper.♾

Book design by Chris Welch

Acknowledgments

We would like to acknowledge the contributions of time, support, and intelligence of Vena Blanchard, Randi Brenowitz, Warren Farrell, Leah Garchik, Bill Henkin, Sandra Leiblum, Jack Morin, Charles Moser, John Robbins, Judith Sherven, James Sniechowski, and David Steinberg. We also thank our agent, Susan Crawford, our editor, Mitch Horowitz, and our publisher, Jeremy Tarcher.

We are grateful to Marty's patients for welcoming him into their lives.

Marty

To the unsung heroes who work to bring
sexual information to the world

Riki

To my parents, Oscar and Harriet Robbins,
who enabled me to manifest my ideas

Contents

Introduction 1

Part I. Intercourse: "Normal Sex," "Real Sex"

Chapter One. Why "Normal Sex"? 13
Chapter Two. Our Normal Sex: Intercourse 33
Chapter Three. Intercourse: Wrong Thing, for the Wrong Reasons 61
Chapter Four. Can Anyone Enjoy Sex That Isn't "Normal"? 88

Part II. Beyond "Normal Sex": Outercourse

Chapter Five. What Is Outercourse? 111
Chapter Six. Advantages of Outercourse 117
Chapter Seven. Beyond "Foreplay," Beyond Intercourse 137
Chapter Eight. Communication Q & A 164
Chapter Nine. The Future of Sex 183

Resources 195
Bibliography 199
Index 201

A Note about Cases

As a Licensed Marriage and Family Counselor and Sex Therapist for nineteen years, Marty has worked with thousands of couples and individuals.

To illustrate our points, Marty has written up some of these cases. To create really clear examples, he has often combined aspects of several different cases. Of course, the names and other details of the cases have been changed to protect everyone's privacy.

Since he's writing from his own clinical perspective, you'll find him saying "I" in these write-ups, rather than the "we" used in the rest of the book.

Introduction

Many people have sexual difficulties. If you're one of them, you almost certainly feel some combination of awkward, inadequate, embarrassed, self-critical, resentful, and ashamed. You probably feel isolated and not normal. And although you want a good sexual relationship with your mate, you feel discouraged, and it sometimes seems like way more trouble than it's worth.

Together, we're going to change that. If you have a regular partner, perhaps he or she will join us. You can even read this book together, or take turns reading it to each other. While that would be nice, it isn't necessary. That's right—although it takes two to tango, you can enhance your sexual satisfaction without anyone else's cooperation.

Sexual difficulties come in all shapes and sizes: problems climaxing; unreliable erections and unscheduled ejaculations; painful intercourse or orgasm; low desire, or desire incompatibilities; self-consciousness about your body or its response; hassles about contraception or disease protection; discomfort about your preferences or fantasies, or those of your partner; and the inability to ask for what you want, or to say no to what you don't want. Other sources of problems include affairs, anger, disappointment, and sadness. Boredom is one of the most common sexual complaints of all.

People also experience sexual difficulties because of physical problems. Cancer (or cancer treatment), diabetes, and osteoporosis can make intercourse impossible. Chronic pain can make intercourse so uncomfortable that it's simply not worth the misery involved. And medication can dry up vaginal lubrication and the surrounding tissue, or make erection difficult or impossible. The truth is, the older we get, the more vulnerable we are to these complications.

Today, there's no lack of guidance for people with sexual difficulties. Here's the kind of advice you may have already encountered—which, with some exceptions, generally *doesn't* work:

- Forget about it—it's all in your head.
- Be grateful for the other things you have.
- Stop worrying—sex isn't that important anyway.
- Focus on being more normal.
- Get your partner to change.
- Have an affair.
- Decide that sex isn't for you.
- Realize that men and women simply can't be sexually compatible.

- Get a new partner.
- Realize you're a "sex addict" or "co-dependent."
- Dress sexier (or less sexy).
- Use your sexuality; tease, flaunt, withhold, or threaten.

And now there's Viagra, the drug that can create erections within minutes. While it does do just that for many men, there are many sexual problems it can't fix. As we'll see in chapter 6, in fact, it can actually make some sexual relationships worse.

Let's be honest: There have been hundreds of self-help books and thousands of magazine articles published about sexual difficulties in the last twenty years. You've probably read a few, perhaps many. Why hasn't all this self-help solved our sexual problems by now?

It's because these books and articles have focused on the wrong things. In fact, *some of this self-help is part of the problem,* reinforcing the feelings, attitudes, and behaviors that cause sexual difficulties in the first place. Self-help that focuses on making you more "normal," or that helps you "perform" better, or that reinforces the idea that sex is intercourse, is no help at all.

This book is different, because it focuses on how you think *about sex*. You'll see how the very ways people think about sex cause sexual problems. You'll also learn new ways to think about sex, and understand how those new ways lead to more satisfying sexual relationships and experiences.

Let's take Mary, for example, a patient of Marty's a few years ago. Her problem, she said, was that she had "lost interest in sex."

"What kind of sex?" I asked the tall, dignified-looking former teacher. "Any kind," she replied simply. "And what kind is generally available to you?" "Lousy sex," she said, a little surprised to hear her own answer. "So you've lost your appetite for lousy sex," I said to her. "That doesn't seem unreasonable, does it?" She quietly agreed. "Go on, please," I gently encouraged. "Why is it lousy?"

"He's like Jekyll and Hyde," Mary said about her husband, a semi-retired engineer. "Foreplay is fine—he's gentle, nice. It's not fantastic, but it's nice. And then . . . and then . . ." "This is hard, I know," I responded to her stammering. "Please continue." "And then, he just changes. He decides that it's time to enter me, and he, well, he doesn't force his way in, but he stops looking at me, stops talking to me, and suddenly it's like we're strangers. And all the good feelings go away." "And you get sad and angry?" I suggested. "Yes, exactly," said Mary. "Sad and angry. And I keep it to myself, because I don't want to interrupt and make it worse, I don't want James to feel bad."

"There are lots of ways to make love," I told Mary. "You already know two; it sounds like you really enjoy one and really dislike the other. Why don't you spend more time with the one you like, and less time with the one you dislike?" "You make it sound so simple," she sniffled, both glad and embarrassed that this was all coming out. "And in what ways is it not simple?" I asked her.

She was silent for what seemed like a long time. "It's complicated when I make it complicated," she announced. "I've been afraid to tell James what I want, because it seems so different from what he wants. Maybe you can convince me that wanting lots of foreplay is normal. That will give me courage to talk with him."

"This may be a surprise," I said, "but I'd like you to make that decision for yourself. It seems to me that you're the one who should decide whether or not what you want is okay."

This turned out to be a longer project than Mary had envisioned. She became angry with me several times along the way. But when Mary finally decided she had the right to choose her own sexual standards, and that they were much more about intimacy and sensuality than "mechanical in-out-in-out," as she put it, her relationship with James changed for good. She even found out his secret: that he rushed intercourse, and had trouble maintaining emotional contact with her during it, because he was afraid of losing his erection. They'd both been withholding crucial information that could have reduced their frustration. And they were both victims of rigid thinking about the supreme role of intercourse in sex.

Making sex less aggravating and more enjoyable is pretty straightforward, once you're able to do certain things. The main one is *reducing your focus on intercourse*. Intercourse itself is connected with a lot of our sexual problems, and many people actually focus on it more than they'd really like to—but they feel obligated to do so. It is a challenge, but you can change this, eventually creating sexual experiences according to what you like, rather than according to what you've been told is "right" or "normal."

You can see how changing her thinking about sex expanded Mary's choices, affected her body's functioning, and enhanced her sexual satisfaction. That's what you can have. Of course, none of us can change our thinking overnight, so we'll go slowly and give you exercises and ideas you can use along the way.

Our goal is for you to enjoy sex more. For various people, that will involve more variety, more relaxation and self-acceptance, more enjoyable stimulation, less anxiety, more desire, more intimacy, and better communication. This *may* result in more orgasms and more dependable erections or lubrication—although, strange as it sounds now, *this won't matter that much*. As you read, you'll find out more about this fascinating paradox.

Our confidence about what you'll be reading has three sources:

1. We've helped many people accomplish these sexual goals before (each in our own professional sphere);
2. Your situation is almost certainly not unique;
3. We propose something different. Yes, this book has something different to offer: a new way of thinking. And this will lead to new ways of feeling and behaving.

To illustrate the pressure that keeps people tied to an intercourse model that doesn't work for them, let's turn to another case.

Joe was one of those sweet, friendly guys who doesn't take himself too seriously. "But," he said, shaking his head and looking at the floor, "my sexual, um, problem sure gets me down. I want to please Aisha more than anything in the world, but I come too fast. And if I don't come too fast, half the time I lose my erection altogether. I would do anything to be the best lover Aisha ever had."

Being "the best lover" is a lot of pressure for any penis to manage. But it was even tougher on Joe than that, because he evaluated "best lover" according to his accomplishments during intercourse. Limiting your sexual repertoire that way is like trying to build a house with one hand tied behind your back.

"How much do you feel in your penis during sex with Aisha?" I asked the short, neatly dressed bus driver. "A little," said Joe casually, as if it were obvious. "And when you masturbate?" "Let me see," thought Joe. "Huh, a lot more." I was silent, letting the contrast sink in. "That *is* interesting," he said. "What do you think it means?" "What do *you* think it means?" I replied, wanting him to start feeling knowledgeable about his own body. Together, we decided it might mean that he was focussing less on his penis during partner sex than during solo sex.

"Is that a problem?" he asked, looking at me. "Oh, now you're going to ask what I think, right?" He smiled. "Well, let's see. I . . . I don't think it's good. I'm cheating myself. But why do I do it? Please, you answer this time."

By session's end, we had discussed his almost obsessive desire to please women by being a "good lover"—and his belief that this required getting and keeping a firm erection. We also discussed my approach to this type of difficulty. It involved focusing on sensations during sex rather than performance, and trusting Aisha enough to jointly custom-design sex with her that they both found relaxing, pleasurable, and intimate. "Whatever it involves," I emphasized, whether it's making out for hours, bathing together, giving each other orgasms by hand, and so on. "When you forget about erections and lasting longer, and *especially* when you forget about being the best lover Aisha ever had, and just focus on having the time of your life," I said, "I believe things will fall into place." And, to make a long story short, he did, and they did.

America the Paradoxical

Many commentators describe America as a sex-obsessed society. But it's paradoxical: the increased sexualization of our culture has not, for many men and women, led primarily to more sexual literacy or more sexual freedom. Instead, it has increased many people's sense of performance pressure; has fostered the belief that everyone else is having fantastic, frequent sex; and has created constant reminders that we don't measure up to these unrealistic standards. In addition, daytime TV talk shows maintain a continual, irrational criticism of many kinds of consensual sex that are commonly enjoyed in private. And they perpetuate an aura of shame around various common sexual difficulties.

In today's America, everyone wants to feel sexually normal. The media, along with fields like medicine, psychology, and religion, talk almost endlessly about what is and isn't sexually "normal." But once you buy into the concept of sexual normality, you're trapped. Other people's ideas about what's right for you become more important than your body's actual experience. And you can never be permanently certified as sexually "normal"; your very next sexual desire, preference, or fantasy could cross one of society's definitions of "normality." Thus, concerns about "normality" keep us feeling permanently insecure and unsettled about our sexuality.

As helping professionals, we do *not* want to help you feel more sexually normal. No, on your behalf we're far more ambitious. We want to help you create a sexual identity and sexual experiences that reflect who you really are, in which you feel comfortable, powerful, and sexy, and able to reach out to a partner when you want to. We want to help you care less about what's "normal" and more about how sex actually *feels* and how it fits in with the rest of your values, goals, and experience.

Us and You

Who are we? You should know whose ideas and experiences you'll be considering. One of us (Marty) has been a Licensed Marriage and Family Counselor and Sex Therapist almost twenty years. The other of us (Riki) has written three books about male-female relationships, and talked about sex and intimacy with millions of people on radio and TV. Male and female, West Coast and East Coast, one of us married, the other not (not at the moment, anyway), we pretty much have all the bases covered.

Who do we think *you* are? Perhaps you're in a rut, looking for some kind of satisfying sexual relationship that you can't quite put your finger on. Maybe age has made traditional intercourse so difficult that you're thinking of giving up sex altogether. Or you may be in one of the many kinds of sexual pain in which humans find themselves these days, and you want support.

If you're struggling with any of these difficulties, you've come to the right place. Throughout the book you'll find stories remarkably like your own, people with whom Marty has worked in therapy. In Part II you'll find specific exercises that will help you resolve various sexual difficulties. Although you may want to skip right to those, we hope you'll go through Part I first. In addition to some fascinating stories, you'll also read about our ideas, vocabulary, and perspective. These will enable you to get much more out of Part II.

We are not the first to articulate some of the ideas at the core of this book. Rather, we see our efforts as clarifying and extending the work that the field of sex therapy has been doing since the early 1970s. Sex therapists Joseph LoPiccolo, Julia Heiman, and Sandra Leiblum were among the first to build on the work of Masters and Johnson, developing new and practical insights into—and treatments of—the sexual difficulties that people brought to them.

Three books of this period were, and still are, extremely influential. Bernie Zilbergeld's *Male Sexuality* explained exactly how performance anxiety interfered with erection and contributed to rapid or inhibited ejaculation. It also challenged the common assumption that sex equals intercourse, and the difficulties this myth creates.

Shere Hite's *The Hite Report* was the first popular book to reveal that most American women do not have orgasms from intercourse alone. Using the actual words of thousands of women, it exposed the unrealistic expectations both men and women had of intercourse, and detailed the frustrations common in sexual relationships that focused on intercourse. It was a huge step toward ending the shame many women felt about their sexual desires and functioning.

In *For Yourself*, Lonnie Barbach described the program she developed to help non-orgasmic women become orgasmic. The program, still used by sex therapists around the world, encouraged women to discover their own unique eroticism, rather than relying on a standard, intercourse-based model of sexuality. It focused almost entirely on various forms of clitoral stimulation—varieties of what we call outercourse.

We believe our book is a fresh way of discussing these important concepts of human sexuality. We hope you—and our colleagues—agree that this book is in the best tradition of sex therapy's down-to-earth, empowering, sex-positive attitude.

There's a wonderful story told about the Danish physicist Niels Bohr, who won the Nobel Prize in 1922 for discovering the structure of the atom. When journalists came to interview him, they noticed a horseshoe hanging above the door.

"Wait a minute," said one reporter. "You're the preeminent scientist of the world, the symbol of rational thinking to millions of people. Don't tell me you believe that a horseshoe actually brings good luck?" "Oh no, don't be silly, I don't believe in such superstitions," replied Dr. Bohr. "But I have it on good authority that it works whether you believe in it or not."

Are you ready to go beyond intercourse? In one sense, it doesn't matter if you are. The program in this book works, whether you believe it or not. So just turn the page . . .

Part I

Intercourse

"Normal Sex," "Real Sex"

Chapter 1

Why "Normal Sex"?

Normal. That's a word people use over and over when talking about sex. Some sexual thing—an activity, a fantasy, a desire—is or isn't "normal." A person—you, your partner, someone else—is or isn't "normal."

Here's how my patients talk about it:

"I masturbate, but I feel plenty guilty about it. My parents and priest have really convinced me it's not normal, especially for a married person."

"She really wants oral sex, but I can't get used to the idea. It's just too weird."

"There's such a big gap between how often we each want sex, it's obvious that I'm a sex addict."

"I have my best orgasms from his hand, and I rarely come from intercourse no matter what he does. We're both resigned to the fact that I'm just not normal."

It's ironic, though. All this "normality" talk obscures a fundamental truth: *Our yearning to be sexually "normal," to have "normal sex" and "normal" sexual desires, lies beneath most sexual difficulties and the emotional pain that accompanies them.*

On the one hand, our culture teaches us that few things are more important than being sexually normal, and that few things are worse than being sexually abnormal. This reflects our society's *"normality paradigm"*—the cultural outlook centered on so-called sexual normality.

Simultaneously, we are taught to question our own "normality"—by advertisers who want to sell us "normalizing" products; the mass media who want to give us "normalizing" information; and medical, psychiatric, and religious institutions that want to fix us, making us "normal." All this pressure leads to our anxiety about not being sexually normal—and that makes it difficult to relax and accept our own unique eroticism.

It's only fair to tell you, then, that this book will *not* help you have more "normal" sex, or improve your ability to make love the "normal" way. In fact, we hope it won't even make you *feel* more sexually "normal." No, our goals for you are much more ambitious. This book is designed to decrease your yearning to *be* sexually normal. Instead, we want to empower you simply to *experience* your sexuality, liking and disliking what you like and dislike without reference to your or others' normality.

Interestingly, as you spend less time comparing yourself to others and to society's ideas of what's sexually normal, as your comfort with your own sexual reality increases and your sense of isolation decreases, you may find yourself feeling *less abnormal*. That's fine with us. But notice that you can feel less abnormal without feeling *more normal*.

Instead, you can focus *beyond* the normal-abnormal continuum—on being present, acknowledging your own truth, and feeling your experience. That's actually what enjoyable sex involves: personal truth, presence, and *involvement* in the experience, rather than *observing and judging* the experience according to some objective or societal standard. We'll explore this kind of enjoyable sex in the second half of the book.

Expanding Horizons

There are many ways to feel sexually inept: trouble with desire, arousal, or orgasm; discomfort with fantasies or preferences; medical problems; dislike of your body; anger, fear, shame, or negative expectations. In our culture, almost anybody facing one of these dilemmas feels abnormal and isolated.

But even some fully functioning people feel sexually frustrated. Many are simply bored. Others feel stuck with the same old partner and wonder what they're missing. Still others fear that their functioning is unreliable, that they'll have a problem the very next time they get into bed. It's an unusual man, for example, who doesn't begin at least some of his lovemaking without any concern about getting and staying erect—even if he's always gotten erect before.

While most sexually frustrated people think the solution is for their bodies to change (that is, to "perform" differently), we disagree. We think, instead, that most people need to expand their erotic horizons. If you're stuck within the model of "normal sex," however, this is virtually impossible. You'd have to try things that you simply *can't* think of within the framework of "normal sex."

That's why identifying and understanding our sexual belief system (or "paradigm") is so important, and why choosing a sexual paradigm consciously is a key step in personal change. As Colorado sex therapist Dr. David Schnarch tells new patients, "To improve your situation you've tried everything that makes sense, right? So if a solution succeeds, it will have to involve something that *doesn't* make sense." Profound changes in behavior or emotions require a serious change in one's belief system, or paradigm.

How do men and women relate to social pressure about "normal sex"? An example of feeling *controlled* is "I wish people didn't make jokes about bisexuality. I'd like to experiment with it, but I couldn't do something everybody thinks is kinky." An example of feeling *independent* of the pressure is "So people think old ladies shouldn't be sexual. Well, I'm sixty-six and still think about sex, and no one's going to talk me out of it!"

What can you do about the pressures to have "normal sex," and the contrast between what "normal sex" dictates and what may feel good to you?

One way for you to get relief from the pressure of the "normal sex" paradigm is to reduce its power out in the world. This would involve political action, such as expanding the sexual activities permitted on TV, or increasing what medical students learn about sex. This kind of activism around sexuality is not a new idea; for better or worse, groups have attempted to shape the definition of "normal sex" throughout history. Examples include the seventeenth-century Salem witch trials and the decriminalization of prostitution in twentieth-century Holland.

Similarly, groups in America with varying agendas have, for the last thirty years, attempted to expand the definition of "normal sex." Different movements have wanted this definition to:

- Include partners of the same sex (i.e., so the definition of "normal sex" doesn't specify "one penis and one vagina");
- Include unmarried people (i.e., the definition doesn't specify "two spouses");
- Include radical age differences (i.e., the definition doesn't specify "people of the same generation");
- Include sex with more than two people or fewer than two people (i.e., the definition doesn't specify "intercourse between a couple");
- Include sex for money (i.e., the definition doesn't specify "sex must not be a strictly commercial exchange");
- Include behaviors that physicians have pathologized (i.e., the definition doesn't specify "people shouldn't get aroused by objects, or by any activity the psychiatric profession has labeled unhealthy," such as playing with pain and control).

A second way to deal with the pressure of the "normal sex" paradigm is to reduce *your desire* to limit yourself to "normal sex." That's what this book is primarily about. To understand our allegiance to these norms from which we feel so much pressure, let's look at the structures of sexual "normality": what makes you so attached to "normal" sex?

The Structures of "Normality"

The definition of "normal sex" varies tremendously from place to place and from one historical period to another. For example,

- There are places in Ireland where, to avoid being immodest or shameful, people do not undress for sex;

- All sex is strictly forbidden for Orthodox Jews while a woman is menstruating and for seven days afterward;
- In medieval Japan, young newlywed couples would have a bedroom helper on their wedding night assist them to have intercourse;
- In Denmark, today's families debate whether kids should wait *until* high school before having sex;
- In ancient Greece, pre-teen boys were considered the partners with whom adult men could have the most spiritually wholesome sex;
- In Russia, rapid ejaculation is considered an expression of passion, not pathology;
- There have always been Pacific cultures in which older men and women are responsible for initiating young teens into sexual activity.

Despite the wide variance in cultural standards of sexual "normality," however, the social and psychological structures that maintain these standards are remarkably similar throughout human communities. The function of these structures is to shape our sexual beliefs, desire, fantasy, and behavioral choices into predictable, socially desirable forms. Let's look at how language and popular imagery shape our sexual thoughts, behavior, and experience.

Language

Language has a double function: it mirrors our inner reality while instructing us in an outer reality. We can't conceptualize anything that we can't describe with words; for example, the Navajo don't have tenses in their language, and so have a radically different concept of what we call "the past" and "the future" than we do. Similarly, anything named with words does exist, socially if not physically; for example, "angels" exist in our minds as a construct, whether or not they exist in the physical world.

We know the Inuit have a dozen words for the many things that we simply group together and call "snow." They make distinctions that have no meaning to us, and so they have words for things we don't have words for. Imagine some isolated group with a genetic defect that makes them unable to see the difference between orange and red, and so they use the same word (*red*) for both. To the Inuit, we are like that group.

Every culture uses words to normalize certain sexual experiences and ideas and delegitimize others. Notice, for example, how the word "slut" applies to females only; there is no male equivalent in our culture. "Womanizer" isn't nearly as nasty and all-encompassing, and "stud" isn't even negative. This perfectly expresses our culture's contrasting attitudes toward male and female sexuality. Here are some other ways language shapes our vision of what's sexually "normal":

- When we talk about intercourse, we say "penetration," not "insertion" or "envelopment." This describes an active person doing something *to* a passive person, and suggests the penis is the most important part of the activity.
- We refer to "getting" and "giving" oral sex, as if only one partner receives and only one gives.
- We snidely talk about "whips and chains" and "S and M," but we have no positive words for the pleasurable experiences of consensual erotic domination and submission.

- The common expressions "premature ejaculation" and "impotence" presuppose an objective standard of getting erections and maintaining them for a certain length of time.
- Our language has many words to describe orgasm (a common product of sex) but few to describe playfulness (a less common process of sex).

Language is one way cultures maintain the concept of "normal" sexuality and patrol its bounds. Recall, for example, that in Victorian England the "breast meat" and "thigh meat" of poultry became "light meat" and "dark meat"—as a way of controlling unwanted sexual passion.

CASE

Sam and His Family

Sam grew up in a home where the nightly family dinner was a boisterous affair. "There was always lots of talk," recalls the ruggedly handsome carpenter, "stories about people and things, stories about the world." Many of the stories revolved around sex in an indirect way. "My father had a name for everybody in the neighborhood, and talked about everyone's sexuality," explained Sam. "Across the street there was Brigitte the Tramp. According to my dad, the guy upstairs from her was Chester the Molester. In our own building there were these Sicilian twins, car mechanics. My dad called them the Italian stallions. And down the block, according to my dad, lived Robin the Fairy."

I didn't have to say much to get Sam to continue. "So a lot of it was about sex. Not practical stuff, like birth control, or wet dreams, or how do you know if you're in love. Just, well, creepy stuff, lots of winking and all these words so full of meaning. We all laughed about it, and my brothers and I would eventually jump on the bandwagon, without even really understanding. 'Yeah, that Robin is a fairy,' I would agree. 'He's lucky he doesn't live in this building or I'd punch him out,' I would say.

"But what did I mean? What did I know? I had some vague ideas, impressions. I just knew that being a fairy was a bad thing, and it had something to do with manliness and sex." The young man winced, his large, callused hands gripping the arms of the chair. Clearly, he wasn't proud of this. "I learned that fairies, tramps, anybody with questionable sexuality—according to my father's ideas—didn't deserve respect. Verbally, we spit on them.

"So I learned that some kinds of sex were good and some were bad. I didn't understand why, and couldn't even articulate what each one meant. But some were good and some were bad. So when I turned fifteen, sixteen, and started having my own sexual experiences, I was nervous. Sure, the usual stuff—not knowing what I was doing, worrying I would look like a schmuck, you know—but also, all this stuff from the dinner table. I didn't want to be a fairy or a molester. I didn't *think* a guy could be a tramp, but I wasn't totally sure. I wanted to be an Italian stallion but didn't know exactly how . . . it was scary." Sam shifted in the chair. I could imagine him as a boy, wanting to make his father proud, wondering if he'd ever be good enough.

"Sex started to seem like it couldn't possibly be worth all this trouble," said Sam. "I became terribly self-conscious. I looked everywhere for clues about how to behave sexually. It got so bad that I'd second-guess myself about dressing for dates, brood about the pitch of my voice, wonder what a girl was expecting, worry how I could be whatever it was she wanted . . .

"I think a lot of the arguments I had with women in those days was a way of avoiding sex, and therefore escaping all these worries about being the wrong kind of sexual person. Also, I was so nervous, I'm sure I took a lot of innocent things the wrong way. I wish I could do it all again, but I guess we all do, right? I'll tell you this, though," he said with complete conviction, "no kid of mine is going to listen, night after night, to stories about sluts and fags and studs and all that crap. It makes you question yourself, worry that you're not okay, scared to have sex because you'll never measure up. I still worry sometimes—does that sexual fantasy mean I'm not okay? Does masturbating like I do make me pathetic? I don't want my kid tormented like that."

Popular Culture

Throughout recorded history, people have been told stories instructing them about "normal sex."

The Greeks and Romans had hundreds of popular stories featuring gods, goddesses, and special humans. Invariably, these beings would engage in sexual behavior considered inappropriate, and disaster would occur.

Some five hundred or more years before that, a small group of people started writing a series of books filled with stories about sexual behavior—some of it legitimized, some of it criticized. We still tell these Bible stories to each other and our children, and still draw lessons from it about "normal sex." An example is the story of Lot's daughters, who, believing they were the last women on earth, seduced their drunk father. Their offspring became the Ammonites, a hated enemy of the Israelites. Another example is

King David, who sent his friend Uriah into battle, planning that upon his death he would marry Uriah's widow, Bathsheba. King David was punished by being prevented from building the Temple of God. And a third example is Onan, who refused to impregnate his dead brother's widow (according to the standard law of Levirate Marriage), and who was struck dead on the spot.

Today, our culture is rich with stories that supposedly explain why the limitations of "normal sex" are both necessary and "natural." News stories regularly feature people who do "bad" things sexually. While singled out for their titillating or bizarre behavior, these individuals are nevertheless considered instructive examples of humans and human sexuality. Common stories you've heard include the teen who gives birth and abandons her baby in a public bathroom; the pedophile arrested with five thousand porn videos; and the gay man who deliberately infects as many people as he can with HIV.

It seems that every popular story about sex is also about disaster: selfishness or passion that destroys families and lives. But why don't we hear a totally different kind of story about sex? For example, we could hear stories about:

- Old people having great sex;
- Couples with large age differences that work out fine;
- Gay couples living happily ever after;
- People with sexually transmitted diseases (STDs) whose sexual lives are mature and fulfilling;
- Satisfied couples whose primary sexual activity is masturbating together;
- Adults who are glad they experimented with many sexual partners when young.

But these stories wouldn't support popular notions of "normal sex."

Like the biblical stories of antiquity, today's urban legends purport to illustrate human sexual nature, using anecdotes based on alleged "facts" that everyone knows but no one can actually back up, things that "should" be true even if they aren't. They are ideas that people hold on to by saying "I don't care about the facts; this idea *feels* true."

Like the seventeenth-century fable of witches changing men into frogs, or the eighteenth-century fable of Jews killing Gentile children to get their blood for Passover matzoh, or the nineteenth-century fable of certain animals having magic powers, or the twentieth-century fable of masturbation causing mental and physical disease, we Americans will take sexual legends with us into the twenty-first century. Requiring no proof in order to be accepted, and resistant to facts to the contrary, these are stories about people who express their sexuality in non-"normal" ways, and who supposedly suffer or create awful consequences.

Here are some contemporary American sexual fables:

- Same-sex experimentation will turn straight people gay.
- Pornography causes people to masturbate and commit violence.
- People who enjoy beach nudity or group sex aren't good parents.
- If polygamy weren't illegal, people would run wild and have sex with every person they met.
- Getting an abortion reduces your future fertility.
- All adult-child or sibling-sibling sexual contact traumatizes children.

These news stories and legends are adult fairy tales—and like children, we take the tales literally instead of metaphorically or mythologically. Now clearly, you're free to dislike any or all these activities. But if you've been repeatedly told that a whole variety of sexual impulses and choices leads to disaster, the *real* message is beyond the specifics—it's about what happens to people who go outside of normal sex.

These modern fables instill fear in us, both of specific activities and of non-normative sex in general. Thus, they make us hesitate to experience and express our true sexual selves, for fear of the negative consequences—even if we know ourselves to be good, responsible people.

The mass media contribute to the process by maintaining a stock ensemble of sexual stereotypes that you have undoubtedly read or heard about: the promiscuous bisexual, frigid housewife, anti-social sadomasochist, predatory homosexual, porn-loving psychopath, ravenous college man, and exploited coed. While many people are trying to eliminate other stereotypes like the cheap Jew, lazy black, and sneaky Asian, there is little support for the elimination of sexual stereotypes. Perhaps you believe one or more of these sexual stereotypes. Why? Are you going on factual evidence, or "just my feelings"? How do you think this rigidity will affect you as you try to enhance your sexuality?

Ultimately, our culture's popular stories about sexuality have two themes: Sexuality is the world's most dangerous form of human energy; and there are sexual predators out there, to whom we're all vulnerable.

In our own era, the popular culture's messages about "normal sex" include: It's for the young and attractive; it's easily distinguished from abnormal sexuality; it's hard for men and women to communicate about; it's embarrassing; one can easily be seduced away from it by those with a perverse agenda.

CASE

The Case of the Missing Ads

The sexual messages of a culture's various institutions are so commonplace that they eventually become completely invisible. Here is a recent situation illustrating this.

In 1989, Good Vibrations, a major retail distributor of vibrators, decided to buy advertising in *Ms.* magazine and *Playboy*. After a great deal of correspondence, both magazines refused the ads.

"To our shock," recalls company founder and health educator Joani Blank, "neither one would take our money—not the magazine that was supposed to be empowering women, nor the magazine that was supposed to be spearheading modern sexuality. '*Ms.* is not a sex magazine,' sniffed *Ms.* 'Our advertising policy prohibits advertising sexual aids,' said *Playboy*. We spent a lot of time trying to get them to take our money, but they simply refused." Several magazines have since changed this policy, but most have not.

According to a recent study by the Lawrence Research Group in San Francisco, several million American households own/use a vibrator. And yet, the American media still assume that vibrators are an illicit item, something to which adults cannot handle being exposed in print. Associated with non-intercourse sex, the vibrator violates taboos that maintain the supremacy of "normal sex." Magazines actually believe their readers will be *insulted* by having information about a common device that enhances sexual pleasure. Thus, *Ms.* and other women's magazines' proud commitment to champion female empowerment, independence, and even sexual fulfillment crumbles beside their far greater commitment to "normal sex"—which they don't even acknowledge.

Relating to "Normal Sex"—What the Good Citizen Does

These various forms of social pressure work. We can see this in the many ways that people relate to the structures of "normal sex"—without consciously planning to.

Most people either behave according to the principles of sexual normality or they think of themselves as "abnormal." While a few people find this exciting, most find it painful. The pain ranges from guilt (mild to severe) to anxiety about being inadequate to fear of being psychologically abnormal to fear of being discovered and judged by one's mate.

While most people admit that psychology and culture shape our sexual choices, we are used to thinking that biology determines our sexual impulses and our physical experience. Yet cultural imperatives shape even these; in fact, for many people, normal sex is the only sex that *feels* good. We learn to devalue our own physical and spiritual experience, letting the culture dictate our actual subjective experience. Many people, for example, reject anal play—not because it doesn't feel good, but because it's judged perverse. In fact, there are people who are ashamed of their mere curiosity about or desire for "inappropriate" forms of sexual expression.

This is one reason that so many women enjoy a penis thrusting in and out of their vagina but are bored by fingers doing the same thing. What they think or believe about "real sex" and "normal sex" actually shapes their physical experience. It's why so many men reject any sexplay involving their nipples—because it isn't "manly," which can be a more salient factor in deciding if stimulation is enjoyable than the actual physical sensation.

In response to feeling pressured about being sexually normal, perhaps you aspire to the "right" physical desires and responses. Many women struggle to have orgasms through intercourse, even though it is difficult or impossible for them (and therefore distracting and sometimes a cause of vaginal soreness). Many men attempt to keep from ejaculating "too soon," distracting them from pleasure and preventing playfulness and intimacy. Berkeley, California, sex therapist Bernie Apfelbaum says that more than performance anxiety, Americans suffer from "response anxiety"—"the irrational fear," he says, "that our bodies won't respond to stimuli that society labels sexy."

In response to the structures of sexual normality, most good citizens cede authority over their own sexuality to culturally certified experts. At various times, these have been clergymen, village elders, shamans, parents, physicians, psychologists, and the mass media; as the cultural beliefs about the source and location of sexual pathology change, so do the chosen experts. As a clinician, I discourage patients looking to me for *the* right insight into their sexuality, which is as bad as looking to Oprah, Ann Landers, or Cousin Shirley for the right answer.

Most good citizens feel abnormal when their bodies don't perform "normally." People don't usually question whether their bodies *should* respond ideally in non-ideal circumstances, nor do they ask if their non-responsive bodies are behaving normally to stimuli they're not considering. Rather, most people think that there's one right way for bodies to perform, and if theirs doesn't, there's something wrong with them. I recall one new patient who came in complaining of erection difficulties. After learning that he had lost his job a year before, that his son was barely staying out of jail, that his wife had gained forty pounds during this time, and that his father had been ill for a while, I suggested that his penis was behaving appropriately by not getting erect. The man replied that I obviously didn't understand the seriousness of his situation.

Good sexual citizens use all the "normalizing" resources they're supposed to. They use language that reinforces the "normality" and superiority of certain kinds of sexuality; for example, we use words like "foreplay," and we say "sex" when we mean "intercourse." And we compare our own bedroom performance (there's another normalizing phrase!) to the standards of normality that "everyone knows" from movies and magazines. People also see sexual functioning (i.e., the behavior of penises and vulvas) as reflecting who a person *is,* not what he or she *does.* This means our whole identity is at stake when our sexual expression is being judged; put another way, we are at risk of being told that not only is what we *do* abnormal, so is who we *are.*

Finally, we bring in evidence to support the local construct of normality. In various times and places, ordinary people will justify the *necessity* for their form of sexual expression (which they themselves may or may not prefer) because it's "natural," "evolutionary," "demanded by God," "other kinds are just perverse," "other kinds have unintended consequences," "it's good for the community," "it enhances relationships," and so on.

In later chapters, we will see how these responses relate to intercourse—*our* "normal sex."

Preferences

From survey after survey, we know that in private, people value many kinds of non-intercourse sexual activity: the orgasm of masturbation, the direct arousal of oral sex, the taboo-breaking of anal sex, the effectiveness of manual stimulation. This doesn't even count things like voyeurism, exhibitionism, sadomasochism, and cross-dressing, which not only aren't intercourse, they aren't even genital (and therefore often not counted in surveys or popular media stories as "sex").

It's interesting (and sad) that given these common experiences, so many people still think they should prefer something else — intercourse. The tension between what you enjoy experientially and what you need in order to feel normal creates despair and dysfunction. To the extent that someone is attached to having "normal" sex, intercourse is the only kind of sex that relieves that internal psychological tension. In that limited sense people do "prefer" intercourse. It is, however, an incomplete kind of "preference." And it shows again how deeply people internalize sexual norms — that we shape our experience around norms, rather than creating norms that reflect our experience.

People with sexual distress often note that their behavior doesn't match social norms, and they want help in changing their preferences or other sexual expression. Instead, good psychologists suggest that maybe people's attachment to the norms needs to be changed, leaving their sexual preferences intact. Patients who can do this can achieve greater results than they ever thought possible.

Reflecting this, here are common problems that bring people into therapy:

- "Even though I'm married, I like to masturbate a couple of times a week. What's wrong with me?"
- "I can't come when we screw, although I come easily from his hand. What's my problem?"
- "Sometimes we get so wrapped up in sixty-nine that we come, and then we're just too tired for real sex. Is that okay?"
- "Sure, I like sex the regular way, but once in a while I really crave her finger in my ass. Am I sick?"

A Heroic Journey

The erotic journey we all need to take is not about erections, lubrication, or orgasm. It's about getting away from the normality paradigm—moving through a jungle of pressured consciousness to a meadow of self-fulfillment.

Wanting to change your attitude toward "normal sex" makes you a hero. That's because you're challenging contemporary cultural—and therefore physical, psychological, and spiritual—reality. You're considering trusting your own experience more than society's meaning-making institutions—which purport to tell you who you are and what's right or wrong about what your body feels and wants. This requires courage, vision, self-trust, and a tolerance for ambiguity. Now, *that's* heroic.

Like a long stagecoach ride west one hundred years ago, the heroic erotic journey includes experiences and challenges that aren't obvious at the beginning—some pleasurable, some painful.

Sexual norms are among the most loudly spelled-out cultural ideals in this and every culture. Whether you're challenging society's sexual norms or its enforcement of them, or simply trying to disengage from the whole apparatus, attempting to live a self-directed, individuated life *is* a heroic journey.

We'll discuss this heroic journey in more detail in Part II.

Chapter 2

Our Normal Sex: Intercourse

ARCHAEOLOGISTS DISCOVER ANCIENT SEXUAL CULT

Archaeologists today discovered the remains of a strange sexual cult with social, political, and religious roots. They were excited to discover its equipment, identify its icons, and decipher its language and mythology.

"Apparently there was a sacred sexual act at the center of this cult," reports a spokesperson. "Most people did other sexual acts, too, but they were considered distractions from, poor substitutes for, or at best mere preparation for the main sexual act.

"This sacred sexual act was continually emphasized

> by the civilization's leaders and elders in medicine, law, religion, and inner-thought science. These institutions encouraged people to hold this sexual act in high esteem, despite its inherent problems. It appears that the common people didn't actually know why this particular act was sacred, but they nevertheless accepted it as such.
>
> "The tribe did have a variety of myths and legends about the special sexual act. These included various versions of a biological mandate (that it was 'natural' and that it brought children) and of what their gods supposedly intended when designing the first man and first woman. But even when various groups transcended this biological mandate because of age, expertise, or physical equipment, they stayed with the Cult."

Sound familiar? This odd-sounding civilization is us, you know, and its cult is our cult—the Cult of Intercourse. Everyone who wants to be sexually "normal" must honor the Cult.

The Cult is important because, without it, people would have to have a different relationship with their sexuality. They'd suddenly have to make sexual choices and decisions with no guidance other than their experience and values. They couldn't say "I'm okay" or "I'm not okay" based on the Cult's ideas about their sexuality—they'd have to decide for themselves. So the *essence* of the Cult (i.e., intercourse) is not the only important thing; the very *existence* of the Cult, regardless of its theme, is important too.

It's no secret: In America today, "normal sex" is penis-vagina intercourse. But not just any old penis-vagina intercourse. In order to be complete and "normal," intercourse has to have certain features. It's supposed to include "foreplay," an "erection," "penetration," "thrusting," one or more "positions," an "ejaculation," and, preferably, one or more female "orgasms." We put these words in quotation marks because they do *not* have objective meanings. They're actually idioms, created to describe a particular activity ("the intercourse we know is normal sex"). We and our social institutions have *agreed* on what these terms mean, and most of us have agreed to aspire to the ideal vision of intercourse (and therefore sex) that they describe.

It's interesting to consider, for example, why everyone refers to penile "penetration" rather than vaginal "envelopment," "containment," or even "grabbing." Each is as accurate as the others, but only "penetration" describes "normal" intercourse. That's because our culture is far more comfortable seeing men as sexual initiators than women.

To be truly "normal," intercourse should also be one's *preferred* method of sex. Other sexual activities should be considered "foreplay" (to prepare for intercourse) or "a little variety" (to enhance intercourse); they're also acceptable when for some reason you *can't* have intercourse (e.g., when recovering from childbirth or surgery), but then intercourse is supposed to resume its central position as soon as possible.

Moderation is a big part of our society's ideal context for intercourse. We're not supposed to make intercourse "too important" or to spend "too much" time doing it. It's okay to dress up for sex a little bit (if you're a woman), but not in "weird" outfits (like leather or drag). Equipment? It may be acceptable to use a mirror if you find yourself in a hotel that has one, but buying one for sex and using it frequently is not culturally acceptable. Role-playing during sex? Something "reasonable" like handsome-duke-&-damsel-in-distress is permissible, but not, say, a man pretending to be a schoolgirl.

"Moderation" describes a "sane" sexuality. It means not losing control of yourself or letting lust take over. Sex, of course, is supposed to be enjoyed—but only on the surface. "Normal sex" decorates or enhances your life. It does not upset, control, or *change* it. "Normal sex" is not profound.

For example, "moderation" as part of "normal sex" means staying sufficiently conscious of what you're doing so that even if you like something that you "know" is wrong—being held down, having your anus stimulated, touching your own penis or vulva—you won't do it. The "meaning" of such activities is supposed to be more important to you than how they *feel*. That means not losing yourself in eroticism, which, of course, limits the possibility of spirituality and transformation in sex.

Thus, intercourse is "normal sex" only insofar as it doesn't threaten society's dominant psychological and political model. "Normal sex" fits into a "normal world." A big reason that people get upset about prostitutes, wife-swappers, and bisexuals is that by refusing to maintain their own "normal" world, they challenge everyone else's.

Creating "Normal Sex"

Our society's authorities, institutions, and media all have well-known views about every aspect of intercourse: what each is supposed to feel like, how our bodies are supposed to behave, where we should not be doing this. Here are some common messages we all get about how to create "normal sex" using intercourse:

Psychiatry: You should be in love with your sexual partner, and that love should trigger your desire.

Most self-help books: Fantasize about whatever and whomever you need to in order to get and stay aroused, or to climax.

Women's magazines: To protect the fragile male ego, it's acceptable to fake orgasms.

"Common sense": To delay ejaculation, think of baseball scores.

Most religions: During sex you should feel intimate with your partner, and not too much passion.

Ann Landers and Oprah Winfrey: Remember, men desire intercourse a lot more than women.

Educational system: Since kids can't have intercourse, they can't have a "normal" sexuality.

This, then, is the "intercourse" the culture means when it names it "normal sex." It is defined *socially* as well as *biologically*. Thus, "normal intercourse" isn't really "natural"; it's the product of a specific historical culture. Other kinds of intercourse—say, group sex, or as part of a church ritual—simply do not qualify as "normal sex" to *us*, even though they have been respected practices in well-known, sophisticated civilizations.

CASE

Johann, Suellen, and the Lube

Suellen and Johann had been married for over twenty years when they came to see me. She complained that they rarely had sex, and then only at her initiation. Johann said he didn't know why he didn't initiate, but that he was glad when his attractive wife did. "I enjoy it whenever we do it," the Austrian baker said with a smile.

Suellen was really angry about being deprived. Johann hated

that she was so hurt and angry about this, and swore that it wasn't personal. "I love you," he said sincerely, "and if I were going to have sex with anyone, it would be you, really."

Either I didn't listen carefully enough in their initial session, or they had been unusually coy (a distinct possibility, as you'll see), because it wasn't until the third session that I became aware that their sexual activity was *exclusively* intercourse. After asking lots of questions, I approached the sex more directly. When Suellen said she sometimes had physical discomfort with intercourse, I offered some sample packets of lubricants. Suellen became really uncomfortable and didn't want them. Nevertheless, I insisted on handing them to the couple, and although she tried to hide it, I could tell she was angry. I made a mental note to find out why.

"How would you two feel if your home assignment this week was to give each other a tour of your genitals?" I asked. "You know, take about five minutes each, and point out your various parts to your mate—your vaginal lips, clitoris, vaginal opening, and so on, Suellen, and your penis, testicles, et cetera, Johann." Behind his wire-rimmed glasses, I could see that the man with the delicate hands felt pretty awkward, but he was also intrigued, and said he'd do it. "Well, I won't," said Suellen, "I'm extremely uncomfortable about this whole thing. Forget it."

I then asked how they'd feel if their homework was to *imagine* doing it. Their response was pretty similar: both uncomfortable, with him willing and her unwilling. "Okay," I ventured, trying to sound cheerful, "how about if your homework is to *talk* about your discomfort about giving each other a genital tour?" Although they didn't like this either, they both agreed to do it. But not quietly.

"Why do we have to have a genital tour?" said Suellen. "He

doesn't need to know everything I have, and frankly, I don't like showing off my body. And lubricants—for God's sake, that's not something people should talk about. Well, not us, anyway. You hand it around like it's candy or pencils or something." Indeed, that's just what I was doing—treating lubricant like an everyday object, and talking about genitals as if they were a regular part of the body. So what was Suellen objecting to?

"I don't want to think about sex," she replied. "Doing it is okay. But you think about it too much, it's not healthy. You get carried away, you want it too much." Ah, we were finally getting somewhere. I asked Suellen to say more. "It's embarrassing," she said, her anger rising as she spoke. "I'm his wife, we have grown kids, I supervise a lot of people at work who look up to me. Is this how a wife and mother should act, playing with sex in broad daylight, moaning or whatever? I don't think so."

And indeed, this is what Johann's and Suellen's case eventually revolved around: her fear of being *too* sexual, her fear that if she were not sober and moderated about sexuality, passion would sweep her away, away from normal sex into something awful like nymphomania. Remember the two or three packets of lubricant I gave her? She described it as my "throwing bunches of stuff" at her—accurately portraying her *experience* of feeling attacked and overwhelmed while inaccurately reporting my *behavior*. For Suellen any old intercourse wasn't "normal" enough; it had to be intercourse that stayed calm, didn't acknowledge itself too much, and was no threat to her sexually conservative self-image.

Are Babies in Charge of "Normal Sex"?

You have probably heard the argument that intercourse is "normal sex" because it's the only kind of sex that perpetuates the species; indeed, some say that baby-making is the only legitimate reason for having sex.

This idea is understandable in societies concerned with expanding their populations, or with high infant mortality rates. Both of these conditions were true for the early Jewish and Christian communities whose sexual values eventually became our own. In addition, the leaders of these early communities were concerned about differentiating their newly forming groups from the surrounding cultures. The Jewish dietary laws of Kosher were one attempt at this, a statement that "*we* don't eat foods that *they* do, and we only eat foods prepared in our special way." One effect of these laws was that Jews could not eat in the homes of non-Jews, an extraordinarily powerful segregator of people 2,500 years ago.

These Bible-era communities developed codes of *sexual* behavior that had similar segregating effects, showing that "*we* don't have sex the way that *they* do." They prohibited many of the sexual practices that were then common in various groups—including group sex, cult prostitution, adult incest, and homosexuality. The frequency and acceptance of these practices in the local population are reflected by the sheer number of times they are prohibited in the Bible. Such sexual behaviors figure prominently in many biblical episodes. For example, the Israelites were frequently tempted to honor Canaanite gods like Baal by having sex with the sacred prostitutes. So when the prophets Hosea and Ezekiel denounced the Israelites for "whoring with other gods," they meant this literally (unfaithful with another person) as well as metaphorically (unfaithful with another god). Sex with other peoples was forbidden to the Israelites. So when, in the Book of Numbers, Zimri is caught having sex with a Midianite woman, they are both killed by Pinchas, who is then considered a hero for preventing the mixed-race sex. The writers of the Bible were particularly determined to show that the Israelites were special, and that this was to be reflected in highly restricted sexual behavior.

Emphasizing procreative sex (i.e., heterosexual, non-incestuous intercourse) was a clever and logical way to discredit the sexual practices of "pagan" neighbors. Early Jewish thinkers were able to do this and be sex-positive at the same time; the Old Testament explicitly describes a married man's duty to satisfy his wife sexually, and old Jewish law says that sex on the Sabbath is a particularly righteous deed.

There were sex-positive early Christian sects as well. But there was a great power struggle among Christian groups in the first centuries A.D., and the winners were those who hated eroticism. In *The Poisoning of Eros,* theologian Ray Lawrence demonstrates that the four hundred years between Jesus and Augustine show a steady decline of the positive sexual ideas of the Hebrews in favor of the sex-negating Greek ideal. With groups like the Gnostics and philosophers like Jerome increasingly favoring abstinence for everyone, by the late fourth century sexual purity was an absolute obsession with the church. It welcomed the thought of Augustine, who stated that sex is the root of human wickedness. He believed that only procreation redeems sexual intercourse—within marriage—so that "something good is made out of the evil of lust."

Over 1,500 years later, the Catholic Church has still not recovered from this position.

And so, even though modern Americans live in a radically different world from that of our biblical ancestors, we still honor a sexual ethic—the primacy of reproductive intercourse—based on ancient social realities.

Today, over 97 percent of the intercourse Americans have is specifically *not* for making babies. In fact, for most people most of the time, the fact that intercourse can lead to baby-making is an unfortunate drawback, not an exciting possibility. Thus, the fact that intercourse is the only kind of sex that leads to procreation can no longer be seen as something that makes it "natural."

Besides, consider what many of us now want from sex, beyond either pleasure or baby-making: intimacy, a sense of being known, a feeling of competence, spiritual fulfillment. As recently as 150 years ago, these were the sexual goals of only an elite group of people. As recently as 1,000 years ago, they were virtually unknown. If we consider that modern humans have roamed the earth for some 75,000 years, the modern goals of sex that we take as "natural" have been felt for only 1 percent of human history.

Sociologist Ira Reiss has a different view of the connection between conception and sexual normality, based on the importance of kinship systems in the smaller human communities of the past. He looks at sex as a culturally defined activity whose meaning is created by social groups, and thinks sex has shaped our view of reproduction, rather than the other way around.

"Reproduction," says Reiss in *Journey into Sexuality,* "has meaning predominantly in connection to . . . kinship and marriage . . . it is not [necessarily] the biological connection of sexuality to pregnancy that is most important [to us]."

Reiss notes that in the past, before people understood the connection between intercourse and reproduction, they valued sex for the way it bonded people to each other, and couples to their families. In some societies, he says, "reproduction can be controlled," whereas in others, "it can be believed to be inoperative." What is much more important to the meaning of sexuality is its physical and psychological aspects.

Reiss suggests, therefore, that reproduction became important because it was an outcome of sex—an activity with powerful social and psychological impact—rather than sex becoming important because it was a vehicle for reproduction.

Today's Social Forces: What Makes Intercourse "Normal"?

Although one of the West's fundamental beliefs about sex is that it is "natural," bodies and biology alone do not completely create our sexual experience. Sexual expression and beliefs are so enormously variable between societies—indeed, even within them—that some other factor obviously helps create the sexuality we each call our own.

That something else is *culture,* socially approved ideas that most people internalize about what it means to be a competent adult male or female. We can see culture in operation if we look at the social forces that transmit beliefs, ideas, and norms throughout society.

As social scientist Michel Foucault says, "Sexuality is the name given to a *historical construct*: a great surface network in which the stimulation of bodies, the intensification of pleasures, the incitement to discourse, the formation of special knowledges, the strengthening of controls and resistance are linked to one another." Or as Ira Reiss says, the way to find "the sources of our sexual lifestyles [is] by looking at our basic social system."

For example, in a society that emphasizes differences between males and females, and between male and female sexuality, intercourse would be considered "natural" sex—because it's the only kind of sex that requires two genders, each with a specialized activity. All other (non-intercourse) sex is essentially genderless, because each partner can do anything the other can, since both have hands, anuses, mouths, etc. That's why non-intercourse sex appears "unnatural" to us.

Here, then, are the five forces in modern American society that maintain our idea that intercourse is "normal sex."

MEDICINE

The medical profession has a long history of involvement with sexuality. The *Kahun Papyrus*, for example, the earliest surviving Egyptian medical work (1900 B.C.), discusses vaginal sores, prolapsed uteruses, erection problems, venereal disease, and pregnancy testing. During the Middle Ages medical thinkers from Asia, Africa, and the Moorish world also made significant contributions to sexual knowledge and practice. All of it was intercourse-oriented, however, from the tantric masters of China to the superstar Jewish physician Maimonides of Spain.

During Europe's secular age, medicine assumed a critical position in sexual thought—based on the assumption that intercourse was the only "normal" form of sexual expression. As Michel Foucault notes, at the beginning of the eighteenth century, "medicine created an entire organic, functional, or mental pathology arising out of 'incomplete' sexual practices, and it undertook to manage them." Medical experts also decided that children's masturbation and sexplay caused "sterility, impotence, frigidity, or the deadening of the senses" in adulthood. The early nineteenth century saw the establishment of "the medicine of sex [as separate] from the medicine of the body," particularly focused on mental problems and the physical effects of impure or degenerate sexuality. Foucault notes that "there was scarcely a malady or physical disturbance to which the nineteenth century did not impute at least some degree of sexual cause."

Doctors today are not usually obsessed with sex. But the opposite is all too often true: today, it is common for a man to leave a urologist's office, or a woman her gynecologist's, without having discussed sex. And to the extent that physicians do discuss sex, the subject is almost always penis-vagina intercourse. For example, urologists are not asking men if they are having anal sex, either as inserters or recipients. Gynecologists are not asking about anal or oral sex, nor about vibrators and dildos. Whether patients have partners or not, few physicians ask about masturbation, much less same-gender experiences. Given doctors' sacred position in the West as the guardians of the normal, moral, and healthy, this omission speaks very loudly.

The AIDS epidemic has forced at least some of the profession to acknowledge and discuss sex. Everyone benefits from the fact that "safe sex" and "use a condom" are now common public health expressions, but this also highlights how heterosexual AIDS education programs are highly intercourse oriented (many schools are prohibited by law from mentioning homosexuality or anal sex in connection with AIDS). That's why most AIDS-education programs preach "abstinence," which is unrealistic, unnecessary, and ineffective.

On the other hand, most sexually active people who think about AIDS and other STDs wonder about the safety of oral sex. And yet a combination of uniquely unimaginative research, the personal squeamishness of many professionals, and a politically motivated refusal to acknowledge the way real people make love keeps the medical field from investigating and discussing this extremely common sexual activity.

Unless they are doing it themselves, how are medical students—tomorrow's doctors—supposed to know about non-normative sex? Physicians are taught nothing about common sexual variations such as fellatio, S/M, or anilingus. In the emergency room, people with problems from anal sex (e.g., punctures of the anal canal or lost objects such as beads) are sometimes told, "If you'd use your rectum for what it's intended for, this wouldn't happen." S/M players who ask questions about pain thresholds, effective cleaning of sex toys, and the physical effects of fetish wear such as corsets and ultra-high heels report being ignored, discouraged, and even criticized by physicians. When Ann Landers says "Ask your doctor," she assumes that doctors will share their knowledge with patients without judgments or withholding. This is simply not the case enough of the time.

One of the most common communication difficulties between health professionals and patients is the instruction to temporarily limit sex (as in, "No sex for three weeks," or "No sex until the sore heals"). Patients rarely know exactly what this means: No arousal? No orgasm? No insertion? No erection? Given this ambiguity, many patients decide it means "no intercourse," which is accurate in only some cases.

The pragmatic problem this creates for most patients is short-term. In the long term, however, the doctor's instructions about "sex" reinforce the idea that he or she doesn't imagine any sexual activity other than intercourse. Most patients will *not* challenge the doctor on this; instead, they'll wonder what's wrong with *them*. At the very least, they'll describe themselves in the *context* of intercourse and "real sex": "I do this *other* thing."

Contrast this scenario with a physician saying "No eating for thirty-six hours" and expecting patients to figure out what this means: No solids? Nothing spicy? No dairy products? No roughage? Nothing in the evening? No medical school would condone such poor clinical work, and few patients would accept it.

CASE

Medicines and "Normal Sex"

Drug companies are guilty of this, too. To pick one example, the patient instructions for Condylox (a highly effective new medicine to remove genital warts) twice warn "no sexual intercourse on days you are applying the gel."

It fails, however, to mention any other kind of sex, such as fellatio, cunnilingus, and masturbation. Given the medicine's intended use—in the genital area—this omission is astounding. It can only be explained by the narrow thinking of those responsible for the insert: the pharmacists and writer weren't thinking like professionals; they were thinking like civilians, living in a world of intercourse. It isn't that the company was afraid of offending customers; "We just didn't think of anyone doing anything besides intercourse," said a company spokesperson. "In retrospect, that's obviously silly." And what about gay men and women—what can they do while using the gel? The instructions don't give a clue. That's because the drug company simply wasn't thinking about non-"normal" sex—which is, in reality, what many people use their genitals for.

CASE

The Embarrassed New Mother

I met Vera about a month after she had had her first child, which was delivered without any problems. A small, attractive woman, herself a psychologist, she was pretty sore after delivery. Her doctor had instructed, "No sex for six weeks," which she dutifully accepted.

"But," she said sadly, "I'm having a lot of trouble. My husband and I are used to making love a few times a week, and we both really miss it." I asked about the range of their sexual activity together and found that they enjoyed a wide variety: oral sex, anal sex, fingers and hands, role playing. "What's keeping you from doing these things?" I asked in a friendly way. The new mother lowered her tired green eyes, clearly embarrassed. "Well, I didn't want to . . . I mean, I couldn't really . . . um, we didn't know . . ."

When Vera felt a little more comfortable with me, she told the story quickly and simply. She had been too shy to ask her doctor exactly what she meant. "We could be happy with just oral sex for a month," she said. "And then anal sex a couple of times just for variety, and to give us that close feeling of him—my husband—being inside me, I want that too. But Dr. Stephens didn't talk about any of this, and she acted like she had covered the subject. I didn't want her to think I was kinky, or oversexed, so . . ." Even a professional like Vera found herself afraid of someone else's judgments about her sexuality.

LAW

As we have seen, by the nineteenth century the medical profession had taken over the definition and treatment of sexual "perversion." In this way, the secularized society transformed sin into sickness, and then into crime. While much of Europe has dropped this idea, it still thrives in America.

For better or worse, current American law views penis-vagina intercourse as a category of sexual behavior separate from all others. For example, "sexual intercourse" is specified as the illegal behavior in both adultery (between people married but not to each other) and fornication (between unmarried people). And in deciding family law cases, courts define "unconsummated marriage" specifically with reference to intercourse, not to sex in general.

On the other hand, in situations where intercourse *is* legal (consensual, of legal age, married, not incestuous, private), sex other than intercourse is often illegal. The prohibited sexual behaviors are most commonly referred to as "sodomy" or "crimes against nature." These terms typically refer to anal or oral sex, and sometimes specifically to same-gender sex, but U.S. Court of Appeals Judge Richard Posner notes that these terms are "not commonly defined in statutory language . . . and the definition may vary from state to state."

"Deviate sexual intercourse" is the other legal term for oral and anal sex, which even the federal Model Penal Code prohibits.

These laws are not ancient; of the states that have sodomy laws, the majority were enacted *after* 1948. And although enforcement has become unusual, it still takes place across the United States.

While these laws do not affect most people's behavior directly, they do exert a subtle influence. For one thing, they are referenced by other institutions—such as universities, the military, and the church—attempting to define "normal sexuality" as they control the behavior of their constituents. They are also part of a system that interlocks with professional psychology, which sees "law-breaking behavior" as a symptom of mental disorders that require treatment.

PSYCHOLOGY

The foundation of Western clinical psychology is Freudian analysis, which since the 1960s has been updated to "object relations theory." This approach explicitly defines the focus of mature adult sexual development as heterosexual intercourse. In somewhat less explicit form, the same is true of most other branches of American psychology, such as gestalt and self-psychology.

Psychologists, psychiatrists, and other mental health professionals typically label non-intercourse sexual activities as acceptable only when done occasionally for "variety." When done frequently they are pathologized as regression, avoidance, denial, and fetishism. A preference for cunnilingus or manual stimulation, for example, is likely to be interpreted as fear of intimacy, discomfort with femininity, compulsive repetition of assumed childhood abuse, even sex addiction. These moral judgments disguised as thoughtful science are unprofessional and dangerous.

Like their medical student counterparts, American psychotherapists get no training in either cross-cultural or non-normative sexuality. Except for their own personal experience, most know almost nothing of healthy sexual variations, spirituality, or transcendence. They don't learn about the use of anal sex to preserve "technical virginity" in certain social classes, or about which racial group is most likely to pursue oral sex to orgasm, or which ethnic groups are so likely to undress and have sex in the dark that they remain uninformed about each other's anatomy their entire lives.

As with medical students, this lack of training maintains and even reinforces professionals' preexisting prejudice and ignorance. It is completely understandable that they would then transmit this to patients, and enshrine it in their books and research.

Psychotherapists, of course, are trained to fit into a patient's world. But when it comes to sex, therapists are not simply mirroring patients' reality; they're mirroring patients' distortions about sex. This is not helpful.

For example, when therapists ask patients about it at all, they typically inquire "how many times per month" they have sex. They use words like "foreplay" and talk about "real sex," "sexual relations," or even "being intimate." Such an approach feeds patients' problems, rather than giving them new ways to understand or explore them. Because when therapists show that they share patients' beliefs that 1) there's such a thing as "normal sex" and 2) that "normal sex" is intercourse, they reinforce the considerable problems caused by this belief—and create obstacles to solving them.

One of the main reasons people come for psychotherapy is the desire to feel normal, and sex is one of the places people most want to feel normal. As a profession, however, psychotherapists should be far more ambitious. We should not cooperate in patients' desire to feel normal; we should be helping people *overcome their desire* to feel normal.

POPULAR CULTURE

FILM AND TV INCIDENCE OF INTERCOURSE VERSUS NON-INTERCOURSE SCENES

While the explicit depiction of genital sexual activity is rare in commercial film, and nonexistent in television, sexual activity is *implied or referred to* almost continuously. When critics complain that TV has "too much sex," for example, they are objecting to the volume of sexual words, sexy clothing, conversations about sex, erotic poses, negotiations about having sex, and passionate embracing that is clearly leading to sex.

This is not the place to discuss whether films and TV should depict sex more or less. Let's ask, rather, why existing sexual depictions or references practically *never* involve non-intercourse sex.

Most Americans somehow have the intuitive sense that audiences would find outercourse "more graphic" and therefore more "offensive." Why would this be? Because, even though virtually all the sexually active audience engages in some form of it, non-intercourse sex isn't considered "normal." In this sense (and *only* this sense), outercourse is less "wholesome."

Another reason for the taboo against non-intercourse sex is the desire for some audience members to deny that people do "those things." Thus, the well-known commitment of both TV and Hollywood to the comfort of the broadest possible audience requires that such depictions be excluded. The media similarly pander to audiences' desire to deny that kids, the elderly, and the handicapped are sexual at all.

Media producers are also aware that in our culture, non-intercourse sex generally represents a level of erotic engagement, creativity, and desire beyond that of intercourse. Since these activities go beyond one's conjugal "duty" and are obviously done "just" for pleasure (rather than procreation), some people consider them "lustful" and even "dirty." The media is hesitant to invite the controversy it believes would accompany references to non-intercourse sex.

In addition to "normal sex," intercourse is considered *generic* sex, so references to "sex" are *assumed* to be references to intercourse. We all collude in this linguistic convention, which is true for polite words—"making love," "intimate relations"—as well as media-acceptable slang—"do the nasty," "spend the night," "sleep with," "get it on." As long as intercourse is generic sex, referring to *non*-intercourse sex will involve specific, *non-generic* language and visuals. This would indeed be uncomfortable for some people. Because intercourse is generic sex, most viewers, if they wish, can hear about it *without* visualizing specific activities; but reference to any other kind of sex almost automatically conjures up detailed images, which is again upsetting for some people.

The work of pioneering media critic Marshall McLuhan helps explain why intercourse is considered more polite than oral sex or other non-intercourse sex. He divided environmental experiences into "hot" (high data, high definition, inviting mere reception) and "cool" (low definition, requiring participation). Radio is hotter than the telephone; trains, which go *through* places, are hotter than airplanes, which go *over* places. Analyzing fashion, McLuhan said that fishnet hose involve the viewer more than regular hose, and slit skirts more than unslit skirts. Our eye acts like a hand to fill in the open spaces, and we experience this visual caress as connective—and therefore "sexy" to some, "offensive" to others.

Extending this analysis, references to "sex" are relatively "hot," its generic meaning (intercourse) requiring little viewer participation to complete. References to non-intercourse sex are "cooler"—they require the audience to participate in completing the unformed image. This demand for participation is exactly what makes some people feel intruded upon. The media have responded by essentially banishing images of non-intercourse sex.

Some observers argue that limiting sexual portrayals and references to intercourse is a media convention, understood by viewers as a stand-in for a broad range of sexual activities (similar to restrictions on films showing or suggesting sex in the 1930s, to which Hollywood responded with kissing as a symbol for sex). We now know, however, that years of such symbolic communication affect people deeply. As a result, many common media conventions have recently been challenged and abandoned: for example, using the word man to mean "generic humans" in print and speech, and using white people to portray "generic people" in films and television. We should see the consistent use of intercourse to portray "generic sex" in the same light — as meaningful and therefore destructive. Intentionally or not, it programs viewers' ideas about sex and, therefore, their sexual behavior.

CASE

MTV and *NYPD Blue*

An instructive example is MTV, the most aggressively sexual of any free TV channel, which carefully limits the depiction of non-intercourse sex. Despite her enormous album sales, for example,

Madonna's 1995 video depictions of light bondage and same-gender sexplay were censored. And though MTV routinely depicts, refers to, and implies intercourse every single day, fellatio, cunnilingus, anal sex, and masturbation (solo or in couples) are dramatically missing. It's as if these activities don't exist in the world of the audience. From this, viewers get a consistent message about what's sexually normal, pervasive, and real—and what is unusual and unhealthy. In the country with the highest rate of unwanted teen pregnancy in the industrialized world, this is a matter of profound importance.

Media producers say that audiences would find references to non-intercourse sex distracting, but this is disingenuous. For information on audience behavior, look at the award-winning dramatic series *NYPD Blue,* which features common street language never before heard on TV. When the show first began, the language was what people talked about; now people who dislike these words have stopped watching, and regular viewers have stopped noticing it—the characters and plot are too compelling.

And yet, with all its graphic language and realism, *NYPD Blue* will *not* show outercourse. And this is actually *un*realistic. Detective Andy Sipowitz (Dennis Franz), who viewers know has had problems with alcohol and sex, would, in fact, have cunnilingus with his TV wife. He would do this to show he cared about her, and, for better or worse, to avoid confronting his sporadic erection problems. He might be embarrassed to discuss it with her, but he would do it. And although we see them preparing for sex and talking about it afterward, it's clear that intercourse is these characters' complete sexual menu.

Think about your "intercourse is normal sex" assumption for a moment. In the next movie you see, in what ways would a visual or verbal reference to, say, fellatio strike you differently than a reference to "sex"?

ROMANCE NOVELS

Romance novels simultaneously pretend that sex is a secret while talking about it endlessly. Tens of millions of romance novels are purchased in this country every year. The portrayal of sexuality and eroticism is a topic of intense emotion and great conflict among both writers and readers of this genre.

In general, the eroticism is portrayed either "sweetly" or "hotly." Experienced readers use a book's title, cover art, and author's and publisher's reputation to select books that will satisfy their preference.

While every romance novel, by definition, features love, passion, desire, and fulfillment, fewer than half portray sexuality in any sort of explicit way, according to Susan Johnson, author of fifteen books. The majority are too sweet to do so. Indeed, according to Johnson, many authors refuse to refer to sex scenes, calling them instead "love scenes." "Many of them contain no sex without total commitment and love," she says, "which doesn't seem realistic. These are more of a fantasy than anything *I* write!"

Debbie Macomber is a perfect example of this type of "sweet" novelist. With fifty million copies of her books sold since 1983, she is one of the most widely read novelists in history. In her books, sex is for married people only. "If two people are passionate but unmarried, I'll have something interrupt them," she says. Even at that, there is genital sex in only about 25 percent of her books. And it's *always* some form of intercourse. As for oral sex or other kinds of sexual stimulation, she says, "Oh, I don't know anything about that, and I don't think my readers want to read about that. As it is, I get letters from readers saying, 'Leave sex where it belongs—in the gutter!'"

According to Louise Snead, the editor and publisher of the romance novel readers' magazine *Affaire de Coeur*, Janet Daily takes credit for introducing oral sex into romance novels only ten years ago. "Before 1988," Snead quotes Daily, "it just wasn't there." And in more than half of all romance novels, it still isn't.

Here is yet another medium in which non-intercourse sex is considered more exotic than intercourse; in fact, it's something that very few heroes and heroines do. Interestingly, these activities could be used to portray the hero as a great, sensitive, patient lover; they could also be part of a woman's sexual awakening, an eternal theme of these books. These books, however, just don't want to show non-intercourse sex.

RELIGION

Western religion is rooted in sex-positive biblical Judaism, which the first two centuries of Christianity transformed into sex-negative beliefs. Western religion now tolerates sexuality primarily as a vehicle for procreation, and therefore recognizes intercourse as the only valid form of sexual bonding—within the institution of marriage.

Modern religion controls the institution of marriage to a large extent: despite today's soaring divorce rates and ambivalence about religion, virtually every marriage in America is performed by a clergy member. By declaring marriage the only legitimate context for sexuality, modern religion gets to contain it. Historically,

Western religion got to dictate what kind of marriage it would accept—monogamous and heterosexual. As Bible scholar Raymond Lawrence and others note, however, nonmonogamy was the norm in biblical times and was accepted in the Middle East during Jesus' lifetime. Obviously, that has changed.

The King James translation of the Bible had, among other things, a particular sexual agenda. Its translation of various stories is now accepted as fact, but the original text clearly shows, for example, that the story of Onan wasn't about "onanism" (masturbation), and the story of Sodom wasn't about "sodomy" (anal sex).

Onan's sin was his refusal to inseminate the widow of his recently deceased brother to provide an heir for his property and name (called a Levirate Marriage). If "onanism" means anything, it is withdrawal at ejaculation. The story of Lot and Sodom explores how far one should go to honor one's duty to be hospitable to strangers. Historian Gerald Larue notes that the word *sodomite* does not appear in the Old Testament; the original passage from Deuteronomy is more accurately translated as "cult prostitute," which the Israelites *did* want to banish from their new religion.

Both the Hebrew and Christian Bibles have been translated to state that heterosexual intercourse within monogamy is the only acceptable kind of sex. Lawrence notes, "As a translation of the Greek 'porneia,' 'fornication' [sex outside marriage, which the Bible did *not* prohibit] is perhaps the most deliberately mistranslated word in the biblical literature." According to Lawrence, "porneia as used by Paul [and the New Testament] meant *'sexual immorality as delineated by the Torah and its subsequent interpretation.'* " Thus, the Bible wasn't against sex or even nonmonogamy; it was against (pagan) cultic prostitution and other prohibited forms of sex.

There is another reason that religion installed intercourse as "normal sex"—the belief that semen itself is magic and should not be "wasted" in non-baby-making activity. Historian Reay Tannahill notes that "Aristotle, in the 4th century BC, thought the fluid semen was a kind of soul substance . . . Galen, 500 years later, said there was no difference between sowing the womb, and sowing the earth; his Christian contemporary, Clement of Alexandria, defined seminal fluid as something almost-man, or about-to-become man. Between them they put a high philosophical premium on semen, which helps to explain why the Church regarded it in an almost mystical light, so that expending it for any purpose other than procreation was a sin in its own right as well as in the more general context of permissible and impermissible sex." Intercourse, therefore, became esteemed because it was the way to be sexual that did not waste precious semen. Asian cultures throughout history have also put a mystic value on semen.

An Intercourse Conspiracy?

Is there an "intercourse conspiracy"? Not in the sense of a conscious, coordinated effort. There doesn't need to be one, because when it comes to sexuality, most social institutions have the same goals—getting people attached to "normal sex," socializing them into a narrow definition of it, supporting normative sex and punishing non-normative sex—so they naturally reinforce each other. In fact, even when institutions have antagonistic missions, they are often willing to get into bed together, so to speak, on sexual issues. This reflects the overriding cultural agreement on the definition of normal sex.

For example, both anti-pornography feminists and anti-choice politicians want to decrease the use of X-rated videos, which many men and women use while masturbating. Both groups attempt to ignore the fact that they differ radically on important issues such as homosexuality and contraception.

On the other hand, our culture's sexual vision is not at all unified. Different sexual subcultures (such as bisexuals, S/M players, and cross-dressers) are developing their own sexual norms, putting them into conflict with mainstream values. One can observe the clash of competing sexual values within American culture in many contexts: prostitution is illegal but is advertised in the yellow pages; universities claim to support women's independence but pass rules to hold men accountable for female students' drinking; teens and pre-teens are given access to contraception but are refused real sex education classes; conservative Christians say they want to reduce the incidence of abortion but will not support teen contraception.

The underlying conflict is about what we know we *are* versus what we think we *should be*. The result is individual behavior and social policies that look schizophrenic. But while there is overwhelming cultural pressure on the side of what we're *supposed* to do, no one with any power lobbies for who we really *are*. In America, people who make sex toys, publish S/M magazines, and run strip clubs have no social standing or political power. They cannot compete with the combined might of the church, medicine, psychiatry, and other "intercourse is normal sex" institutions. And consumers of these services rarely stand up for their rights as sexual citizens, fearing their community's judgments.

So for today's Americans, "normal sex" is, overwhelmingly, intercourse. What's the problem?

Chapter 3

Intercourse: Wrong Thing, for the Wrong Reasons

In chapter 1 we established that most of us want to have "normal sex," and examined the problems resulting from our "normality anxiety." In chapter 2 we saw how most Americans believe that "normal sex" is intercourse. Looking at the nature of intercourse, we will now examine the problems created by this belief.

Americans complain about intercourse regularly. Of course, most people don't phrase their feelings as "complaints," but if you listen with a careful ear, that's what you hear.

It sounds likes this: "Sex would be okay, except when X happens (losing an erection, fumbling for a condom, worrying about not climaxing, etc.). Then sex is a problem (difficult, embarrassing, impossible, etc.)."

Interestingly, most complaints about sex are true only insofar as people are attached to intercourse. People may *think* they're talking about "sex," but they're really talking about *intercourse*. If people weren't so committed to intercourse, most of these situations and frustrations would go away. These complaints also depend on people wanting to be sexually "normal," which, as we've seen, is one of the main reasons people are so attached to intercourse.

Complaints about intercourse fall into two categories: what it *actually* requires and what it is *supposed* to be like.

Intercourse does, of course, have certain requirements: an erect penis (regardless of how it gets that way), receptive vagina, and lubrication (natural or artificial) sufficient to permit insertion. Of course, these are requirements of *intercourse, not of sex*; to the extent that we confuse sex and intercourse, however, they become requirements for sex as well. On the other hand, if we don't confuse the two, the lack of one or more of these conditions doesn't prevent sex; it simply means that you can't have *intercourse* (which in itself isn't a problem). Note that any "requirements" for intercourse other than the three named above are either cultural standards (such as privacy) or personal preferences (such as being in love); the fundamental nature of intercourse does not demand them. What conditions do *you* prefer for sex?

While human *biology* is more or less fixed around the globe and through the centuries, human *attitudes* about what intercourse should be like exhibit amazing variability—and every culture has norms about this. In Victorian England, intercourse was supposed to be extremely unpleasant for middle-class women; for the pre-Manchu Chinese, intercourse with more than one woman in a night was most spiritual; an ancient Assyrian, Hittite, or Bedouin widow was supposed to do it with her brother-in-law to help perpetuate the family name. In today's Russia, it's supposed to be quick; in Japan, quiet; and Chasidic Jews around the world may not do it during menstruation.

Most people's ideas about intercourse are culturally shaped beliefs, often at great variance with their personal experience. But individuals must take responsibility for accepting cultural ideals, whether about fashion, ethics, gender, or anything else. People who complain about how disappointing it is not to live up to the way intercourse is supposed to be and who respond by depriving themselves of sex are like people who accept obscene phone calls collect and then complain about the bill.

Living in a mechanistic, goal-oriented culture makes our sexual myths understandable, almost inevitable. The result, however, is that intercourse is seen as performance-based, rule-governed activity. That means, unfortunately, that there are ways to fail at it. Compare that to, say, cuddling or kissing, where there's no right way to do it, there's no goal, and the only way to evaluate it is by referring to the enjoyment of the participants.

Because intercourse is society's official sex act, there is an aura, a kind of psychological field, surrounding it. Most people who engage in intercourse enter a sort of cultural trance. This is even true, as veteran sexuality educator Vena Blanchard says, for many people who are comfortable during non-intercourse sexual activities. In this trance, the mythology around intercourse overshadows the actual experience. We believe arbitrary ideas about it and accept society's rules about it. And we believe that if our bodies and minds don't conform to these cultural standards for intercourse (e.g., "external lubrication should be unnecessary"), we, rather than the standards, are inadequate.

So let's turn to people's complaints.

First we'll address people's complaints about how intercourse actually is, and the resulting consequences for people attached to intercourse: that they can only have sex under narrow conditions or by taking risks that are extremely serious—far more so than they would typically risk in other parts of their lives.

• The erection determines when sex begins, ends, or is possible. *"When I/he lose my/his erection, sex is impossible or over."*

People joke about men being led around by their penises. Well, here's a situation in which almost *everyone* is being led around by a penis—their own or their partner's.

Intercourse *requires* an erection, whether it is generated through physical stimulation, fantasy, a mechanical device, or drug (injected or ingested). And since for most people sex equals intercourse, the lack of erection means sex is impossible.

This arrangement appears to give great power to men, who own the penises. Interestingly, however, this is not how they generally feel. Many men experience the one-sided arrangement as a burden, not a privilege. Similarly, although many women feel frustrated about having to wait for a penis to become erect before they can have intercourse, they are also free of the performance pressure that many men resent so much. Few couples talk about this dual dynamic—the pressure to perform versus the anxiety of waiting, and the power of being the initial actor versus the comfort—and unique pressure—of the responder's role.

Many men get erections when they desire, only to lose them during erotic activity. Obviously, if sex is intercourse, a lost erection is the end of sex. As a result, men and women who are anxious about losing erections often hurry during sex—they hurry to get to intercourse as well as to finish it.

This makes it harder to actually *feel* and be captured by the sexual stimulation. Ironically, this increases the chance that the erection will subside, as feared. People who rush simply can't get as much of what sex has to offer; they can't feel as connected with their partner, and can't verbally communicate as well as they might.

The key to good sex is not erections; it is being present. Admittedly, "showing up" takes a certain kind of consciousness. Paying attention to the sound of your partner's breathing may not intuitively sound as satisfying as working hard to keep an erection (whatever that hard work might seem to consist of). Yet in sex, there is simply no substitute for paying attention—not obsessively monitoring the environment but simply being there, available, open, breathing deeply, feeling what your body feels.

Erections are involuntary reflexes, like sneezes. Would you put a sneeze in charge of your sex life? Probably not. What about a nose? Not dependable enough. Putting erections in charge of your sex life is like putting the barbecue grill in charge of your eating life. Let's say the barbecue usually works fine, but it does need charcoal and time to heat up, and it's sometimes finicky. It also has limitations regarding unpredictable rain and cold winter weather, and there are foods (like oatmeal, quiche, and chicken soup) that you can't cook on it. No, you'd use a barbecue as *part* of your overall cooking/eating routine, rather than centering your food life on it. The same is true for erections: it's lovely to include them as *part* of your sexual routine, but whether you're male or female, it's extremely limiting to center your sex life on them.

Notice we're not talking penises here, just erections. Penises are fine whether they're firm, limp, or in between. Sometimes you can use them for intercourse, other times not. You can almost always use them as part of sex. If you want to.

CASE

Martha and Marv

Martha enjoyed many sexual activities with her husband, Marv, in addition to intercourse: kissing, caressing, and reading sexy stories to each other, all of which they considered "foreplay." But Marv started having erection difficulties. Although these various erotic activities were still completely available, Martha soon became so anxious about the question of intercourse that she lost her ability to enjoy them. In fact, after only a few minutes of sexplay, she would rush them to intercourse, even though neither of them was ready. The quality of their overall sex decreased a great deal; in Martha's mind it was because of Marv's erection problem, but she needed to understand that it was because of her attachment to intercourse and her anxiety about losing it.

- Ejaculation determines when sex ends.

"When I/he comes, sex is over."

When is an erection not an erection? When it explodes. Except for unusual circumstances, all adult men have a refractory period after they ejaculate—the waiting time the body needs before it can get another erection. In the overall scheme of things this need not be a problem, the same way that other body rhythms are no problem as long as we respect them: we have to wait after a heavy meal before exercising; we have to wait after we first wake up to think clearly; we have to wait after coming in from a bright day before we can see in a dark room. As long as we don't try to ignore these rhythms, or assume they won't happen this time, or think they indicate a problem, these rhythms don't disturb us.

But if you believe that sex equals intercourse, the refractory period—which temporarily ends the chance for erection—means that ejaculation signals the end of sex. And that makes people nervous about when they or their partner will ejaculate—specifically, "too soon." This is a special version of erections controlling people's sex lives.

People cope with this concern in a variety of ways:

The man tries to prevent ejaculation, typically by reducing his enjoyment of sex.

The man pretends he hasn't ejaculated and continues intercourse after orgasm; this is typically unpleasant and can only be done for a short while.

The man pretends he hasn't ejaculated but stops intercourse for some other supposed reason.

One or the other partner won't have sex, and won't say why, or says it's "too frustrating."

The couple has the woman orgasm before intercourse, reducing the importance of when the male ejaculates and loses his erection.

Needless to say, if a couple has many ways to be sexual together, an ejaculation doesn't have to end sex any more than a sore hand or tired mouth does. Of course, if people thought that "normal sex" was, say, cunnilingus, a tired mouth would be a serious problem, and people would be arguing about whether or not someone's jaw was adequate.

CASE

Herb, *Almost* the "Perfect Lover"

Herb knew what women wanted (or so he thought): intercourse and plenty of it. He was a gentle and generous lover, but he was very concerned about ejaculating too quickly. Therefore, he focused much of his attention during sex on not climaxing. As a result, his partners thought of him as well-intentioned and skillful but emotionally withdrawn and distant. They didn't know if the problem was that he didn't find them attractive, or that he didn't like sex with them, or that he was thinking about someone else. Poor Herb—so close to being the lover he wanted to be, but so far away. If he could only believe that his partners were more flexible than he feared, and if he could focus more on enjoying himself and less on doing sex "right," he could relax and have the sexual experiences he really wanted.

- Genital health controls whether or not you can be sexual.

"A herpes outbreak/yeast infection/other STD means no sex."

Remember when many people thought herpes was just about the end of the world? The feeling seems almost quaint in today's world of AIDS—not to mention that millions of baby boomers now have it. While many men and women are managing their herpes very well, others are being quite self-defeating about it.

Despite its almost routine appearance, however, shame about herpes is still common, as is embarrassment about vaginal and bladder infections. Responsible people won't have intercourse when they or their partner has an active outbreak of any sexually transmissible condition—and so for some large number of people, active infections mean no sex.

Many kinds of sex are typically available to contagious infected persons and their partners (unless an infection makes stimulation and excitement just too physically uncomfortable). Unfortunately, embarrassment, poor communication, anxiety, and, most of all, narrow thinking about "real sex" make non-intercourse sex unlikely under these circumstances. People often get angry that their infection has "deprived" them of sex. But it's not true—it's *beliefs* about the meaning of sex that deprives people.

Of course, some people take a *big* chance and have unprotected intercourse. Again, this is a much bigger risk than the nonsexual chances those same people typically take.

CASE

Myra and Herpes

About three times per year, Myra had a herpes outbreak. She certainly didn't want to pass it on to her partner; on the other hand, she didn't want him to know she had the disease. This meant that there would be times when she wouldn't be able to have intercourse, which she was afraid a man would find unacceptable. So there were times when Myra declined to be sexual, letting her partner think she just wasn't interested. She didn't trust that her lover could handle the periodic lack of intercourse, or that they could at least talk about it and manage his disappointment (not to mention hers). Her attachment to ideas about intercourse ("men have to have it") was bigger than her trust in her partner.

- Chronic pain or weakness in certain (non-erogenous) body parts controls whether or not you can have sex.

"I feel too much pain/weakness in my knees [or back, or elbows, etc.] to have intercourse; therefore, I can't have sex."

For better or worse, intercourse is more than putting tab A into slot B. Although almost no one talks about it, intercourse also involves the flexion and weight-bearing of knees, hips, shoulders, elbows, and wrists. There are no large joints that are *not* heavily stressed during intercourse, whether for a few moments or the entire activity.

Tens of millions of Americans have joint pain, either chronically or occasionally. As a sexual issue, it is generally ignored by physicians, artists, and advertisers (I'm waiting to see the commercial "Sore back? Two Tylenol with that candlelight dinner will make sex more enjoyable later"). As a result, many people with chronic pain feel isolated and inadequate regarding sex, and may not do what it takes to maximize their sexual satisfaction.

One of the things they need to do is create an erotic style that accommodates their limitations. This may mean limited thrusting, or emphasizing what the Eastern traditions call "peaceful positions."

For people with joint pain, exploring non-intercourse sexual activities is particularly appropriate. Judaism has a law called *pikuach nefesh* that dictates, "If it would hurt your health or family to follow one of God's commandments (say, fasting when you're sick, or going to synagogue when your baby needs you at home), don't do it." We need a similar *cultural* rule that says, "If sex a certain way hurts, don't do it—even if it's the 'normal way' and you really want to feel normal." This would help chronically hurting people who are highly attached to intercourse to feel more comfortable exploring non-intercourse alternatives that they could actually enjoy.

Note also that our culture's emphasis on intercourse and the reality of the body's aging process also means that "sex" supposedly becomes less and less available as we get older.

CASE

Oh, My Achin' Back

Joe's back was bothering him more and more. When the weather changed, or he had a really difficult day at work, or he spent too much time gardening, he especially hurt. But he didn't want to disappoint his wife in bed. And he "knew" that intercourse was the only sex that really counted. So rather than tell her he couldn't get on top of her as he used to (the only position they both felt was "regular"), or require her to "settle" (as he put it) for other kinds of lovemaking, he simply withdrew from sex. It wasn't a conscious decision; his sex drive simply declined. He just wasn't in the mood, he increasingly found. He attributed it to age—but at fifty-one, he was hardly an old man.

• The need for protection against conception and disease controls whether or not you can have sex.

"Contraception is an interruption and 'unnatural'; my concerns about it are an imposition on my partner."

This news bulletin just in: Intercourse can lead to conception, pregnancy, and even children. And while there are various ways to interrupt this chain of events, the consequences are pretty predictable if you don't.

Interrupting the chain effectively, however, involves more than simple mechanical actions or technical expertise. It requires acknowledging that you're engaging in the activity whose consequences you want to interrupt, and admitting that this is the person you're doing it with. Unfortunately, too many people simply don't want to acknowledge they're being sexual, or that they're actually being sexual with the person they're with. Furthermore, many methods of contraception require communication, which some men and women find uncomfortable.

Therefore, dealing with the fact that intercourse can lead to conception is far more complicated than selecting a contraceptive method. For many people, in fact, the technical side is the easy part, while the emotional and communication aspects are the tough part. Kristin Luker discussed this in her groundbreaking book *Taking Chances*.

One problem is that many people feel that caring about conception is somehow unseemly, unromantic, not sexy, and intrusive. This is like going to a restaurant, and in order to enjoy a nice meal, needing to deny that a kitchen prepares the food, which it gets from delivery trucks, which get it from wholesalers, which get it from factories or farms. While this thinking—that birth control is unromantic—seems intuitively obvious, it's actually just the opposite. Separating out one part of sex—contraception—and making it *un*sexy requires a big effort. This effort is socially supported, of course: movies and other cultural images of "great sex" (which means, of course, intercourse) never mention contraception, so it never seems like an integral part of sex.

And since our culture doesn't say much about the "normal" desire to want to contracept, or the "normal" negotiations most couples go through about birth control, many people actually feel that their concern is unreasonable, an intrusion on the "spontaneity" of sex.

Contraception unsexy? Intrusive? This is just a misunderstanding. I ask high school guys, for example, "You mean if Mariah Carey said, 'C'mere, let me bite your ear and put this condom on you so we can make love,' you'd think, 'Ugh, how unsexy'?"

Finally, the other response to the reality that "real sex" (intercourse) can lead to conception is unprotected intercourse, a level of risk that few people would take in nonsexual situations (many people who have unprotected intercourse use seat belts and safety goggles, drink bottled water, tear up their credit card carbons, and wash their hands after using the toilet). Incredibly, there are people who feel they have no choice about this: that their partner, or their erection, or their church would not tolerate either birth control or non-intercourse sex. This is quite sad.

CASE

Protection or Perfection?

Nancy returned to the family-planning clinic for the second time in four months, this time for a pregnancy test. "Didn't you get a diaphragm the last time you were here?" asked the nurse practitioner. "Yes," the college senior replied. "And how is it," asked the professional as gently as she could, "that you might be pregnant?" "Well," said Nancy, looking around the room, "I have this new boyfriend. About three weeks ago we came back from a concert, started fooling around, and got really excited. It was wonderful.

When it became obvious we were going to have sex I knew I should get the diaphragm, but it was our first time and I didn't want to interrupt us, I just wanted it to be perfect. . . . He looked at me and said, 'Wait, what's the deal with protection?' I know we could have just done, you know, oral and other stuff, but I just wanted it to be perfect. So I . . . well, you know . . ."

So Nancy had "perfect sex"—intercourse—without contraception. Now she's scared to death. It didn't have to be that way.

Summary

Intercourse has built-in problems that many people try to ignore. In doing so they typically undermine their sexuality, or take risks whose consequences undermine their lives. That's bad enough. But we make things worse, as described by the group of issues discussed below.

More Complaints

The second group of complaints about intercourse relates to concepts of *how it's supposed to be,* and people's laments about how far someone's body or mind is from the ideal situation he or she really believes in.

Everybody knows what intercourse is supposed to be like. We can all agree (more or less), because we're not talking about facts or personal experience; we're talking about a cultural ideal. It's similar to the way everyone in a given culture can describe a beautiful mountain, even if he or she has never seen one—there'd be some variation, but everyone would cover the same basics. So the fact that everyone knows what intercourse "should" be like doesn't indicate anything real, just a consensus about an ideal.

Isn't it interesting that this ideal on which we all agree is so different from our own experience? What does that mean?

- It shows that sex is a culturally mediated activity; regardless of what our bodies tell us, sexual expression means what our culture says it means.
- It's obviously the *ideal,* but people forget that and imagine it's how sex *should* be. Confusing an ideal with an expectation is a big mistake.
- It means we may have to choose between honestly acknowledging our experience and the gratification of feeling normal. This is extremely painful for many people, leading variously to secrecy, anger, dysfunction, blame, performance anxiety, and withdrawal from sex.

What else does this mean?

It means that the more you desire to feel sexually normal, the less control over your sexuality you have. We're obviously vulnerable to manipulation regarding our would-be sexual "normality," and we therefore give various cultural agents the power to set our sexual agenda. These agents include the advertising industry, organized religion, the law, the medical profession, and our partner.

It also means that we don't take our own experience seriously, that we disempower ourselves by seeing sex as a left-brain (logical, succeed/fail) rather than right-brain (nonlinear, artistic) activity. Given our sexual ideas, of course, virtually all of us are destined to "fail"—and to blame ourselves and sex, not the unrealistic cultural standards we try to attain.

Just as all cultures have ideals about how their citizens should live (ideal weight range, family size, personal hygiene, health, "normal" pets, etc.), so cultures have explanations for why some people fail to achieve cultural ideals. These explanations almost always focus on the shortcomings of the individual. We can see this in our culture's explanations of Americans' weight problems (moral weakness, dysfunctional family), the high American divorce rate (lack of religious influence, feminist movement, men are jerks), and the low American savings rate (hedonism, weak nuclear family).

As would be expected, our culture has generated explanations for why any given individual's sexual expression doesn't measure up to the intercourse ideal—that that individual is or was:

- from a dysfunctional family
- a sex addict
- latently homosexual
- "promiscuous"
- afraid of intimacy
- "frigid"
- expressing postabortion trauma
- molested as a child
- too old
- a pervert
- a lousy lover
- guilt-ridden
- dealing with a "medical problem"

Nobody really wants to think of him- or herself in these ways. Thus, people find themselves in a bind when they don't measure up to society's sexual ideals: either they are incompetent or unhealthy in some way, or their partner is. A lot of the blaming and judging I see couples do is simply defensive, expressing the feeling "I don't want to be the sick one, so I guess you'll have to be." This, of course, pulls the other partner right into a conflict. It would be nice if people could say, "I feel inadequate or alienated from our culture's sexual standards and vocabulary, even though I think I'm okay. Can you work with me to create sex that may not look picture-perfect, but which we both enjoy so much that we can ignore its nonconformity?" Unfortunately, some people see even this conversation as evidence of "intercourse failure." And that, of course, comes from one more societal ideal of intercourse — that no serious talking should be necessary.

Let's examine a variety of tangible ways in which the ideal of intercourse affects us. We'll look at the contrast between people's personal experience and cultural ideals in areas such as orgasm, "foreplay," birth control, lubrication, pain, time, planning, and preferences. While this list isn't exhaustive, it does show the wide range of ways in which our loyalty to intercourse affects our sexuality.

- The intercourse imperative controls whether or not people orgasm.

"I don't come from intercourse and I/my partner won't or shouldn't do other stuff."

Orgasm can be a delightful part of erotic activity. In reality, the orgasm reflex can be triggered by almost anything, as long as the body and mind interpret it as pleasurable. Unfortunately, many people squander this potential by limiting their orgasmic opportunity to the stimulation they can get from intercourse.

For most women, this is a problem; stimulation of the clitoris (*not* the vagina) is what ultimately takes them over the orgasmic threshold, and intercourse alone rarely provides that. Therapist Lonnie Barbach says many women unrealistically expect a "Look, Ma, no hands!" orgasm. For men, too, reliance on intercourse for orgasm is problematic: anxiety can make erections undependable, physical stamina is important, and it's difficult to control the exact stimulation received.

Nevertheless, many people feel that intercourse is the right way to have an orgasm (some insist on the couple climaxing from intercourse simultaneously, a feat only slightly more complex than landing a spacecraft on the moon). If that doesn't do it, they feel they must go without. In truth, hands, mouths, nipples, anus, and toys can be the center of orgasmic sex. What a shame to ignore these possibilities by focusing strictly on intercourse.

CASE

"I Don't Climax"

"Please fix me, I don't climax" were the first words Rebecca said at our initial session. Her husband, Hector, was obviously sympathetic, although he seemed uncomfortable with his wife's candor. "Yes, we love each other," he said boldly, "and we desire each other. I want to satisfy Rebecca, but . . ." His words trailed off in embarrassment. "I last as long as I can, but it doesn't seem to matter."

I pulled out my trusty old drawings of female anatomy and gave them a simple lesson. ". . . And so that may be the main reason you two are having this difficulty," I concluded. "So women don't climax from sex?" Hector was confused, and blushing a little. "My girlfriend before I got married seemed to." "Some women do climax from intercourse, but most don't," I gently replied. "Most women can orgasm from some kind of sexual stimulation, though, whether it's from a partner's hand or mouth, her own hand, or a vibrator. So you two need to experiment and find out what works best."

"So it's possible I can have orgasms from sex, if we figure out how?" asked an excited Rebecca. "Are you sure this is like how it is for other couples?" asked an anxious Hector. I framed their situation as a wonderful marital opportunity, and they left the office. I heard from them only once more, about three months later—when I received a postcard from their "second honeymoon" in San Diego, where they went to celebrate their new sexual relationship.

• Correct intercourse needs no planning or communication. *"Intercourse should be natural and spontaneous; otherwise, I feel clumsy and unromantic."*

What a wonderful fairy tale we all absorbed while growing up: that proper, satisfying sex should just "happen." And how unrealistic to think that anything as complex as two people taking off their clothes and undergoing physical, emotional, and spiritual transformation should happen without communication, planning, or any awkwardness.

Communication and planning make spontaneity possible: when you have your supplies, a basic understanding of what you both enjoy, and trust that you can talk and direct things any way you like, that's when you can relax and allow your body to take over, letting the feelings wash over and change you.

CASE

Joanne the Frazzled

Combine a part-time job, two young kids, an elderly mom who lives nearby, a church committee position, and a new German shepherd puppy, and what do you get? "One frazzled lady, let me tell you," said Joanne, who looked like one frazzled lady. "Sex? When? I haven't had a full night's sleep in four years." She laughed. "Besides, John—God love him—is the least romantic man you could ever meet."

John obviously loved his wife and was very unhappy about the lack of sex. A practical man, the good-looking carpenter had tried everything—including making dates for sex. This was the last straw for Joanne, who then agreed to counseling. "Can you imagine—making a date for sex!" Joanne said, shaking her head. "Then what, we think about it all day and get into bed like robots on a mission? No, thanks. Sex should be spontaneous, unrehearsed."

"That's the kind of sex you're having right now," I said gently. "But we're having hardly any sex," Joanne snapped in frustration. "That's the point," I replied. "Your lives are so crowded that without planning, it's almost impossible to just find yourselves lying around with nothing to do, and then you look at each other and jump into bed. And if you wait until the last thing at night before going to sleep . . ." "We already know how that works," said John. "One of us falls asleep while the other yawns and tries hard to be sexy."

"Exactly," I said. "So how about if every week or two you guys make a date to be available for sex? You don't necessarily have to have sex during your date, but at least you'll plan to be in the same place at the same time, with privacy and no other responsibilities. Then if you want to make love you can. If you don't want to you don't have to, but you do have the option. That will give you a lot more flexibility than you have now."

• The model of "correct" intercourse makes my body wrong. *"To have proper intercourse, I have to deny my body's reality."*

For many men and women, there's intercourse, and then there's intercourse correctly done. Many people think, for example, that "needing" to use a lubricant is some kind of weakness, an unnatural addition that diminishes sex. They feel that the fact that their body may want some extra lube, or that extra lube makes the sex better, is irrelevant in the face of social standards of "correct" intercourse.

Most adults have many experiences like this. Examples of other times a body's needs may clash with how intercourse is "supposed" to be include:

Having to stop to go to the bathroom
Wanting a partner to shave, shower, or brush his or her teeth
Needing to stop to catch a breath, or to change positions to relieve a cramp
Needing to avoid certain positions because of chronic pain
Passing gas or urine during sex
Limiting vigorous sex to early morning or some other time because of biorhythms (as affected by age, medication, or personal comfort)

Denying your body's reality and needs in order to have correct sex is like denying your body's nutritional needs in order to eat what's in fashion—and then complaining because you get sick or feel hungry. Don't blame your body for having its own needs, or for having needs that contrast with social ideals of intercourse. Our bodies are always wiser than our culture—especially regarding sexuality.

CASE

Camille the Damp

Camille genuinely enjoyed sex. There was only one catch: Over the last few years, she'd begun wetting the bed a little when she was really excited. And she couldn't stand it.

There was no one she would talk to about it—not a physician, not her husband, not her sister, no one. She only called me when she saw me speak about it on TV. But she cautioned me on the phone: "I'll come in, but you have to promise to take this seriously."

"It's getting worse," she said after we had spent some time together. "And now I'm having trouble coming, which is driving me crazy." Camille had had this experience (I refused to call it a "problem") for years, but it was increasing with age. I explained the physiology of the vagina, uterus, and bladder and explained that she was probably dribbling a little urine, which her body might do more frequently as she became older.

I described a series of exercises she could do to strengthen her pelvic muscles. "This probably won't prevent a little trickle every now and then, but it very well may keep it from increasing in volume over time," I said. After we discussed this awhile, I suggested we talk about orgasms. Camille didn't understand why it was getting increasingly difficult to climax. I asked her to tell me what it was like to get increasingly excited, knowing she might drip a little if she became really aroused. "I start off fine, I like the way Bernard makes love to me," she said. But as she talked about her experience, her entire body became tense. "Camille," I asked gently, "do you do anything to keep from dripping during sex? I wonder if you're tensing your belly, or turning your hips in just a little, or doing anything else without knowing it." I stood up and demonstrated on myself, exaggerating things a person might do to keep control of herself.

And Camille started to cry. "Yes, I can tell that that's what I do. No wonder I have trouble coming! Now what do I do?" she cried. "Now frustration on top of embarrassment!" "There's a limit to how much you can control your body," I said. "But you can change your attitude toward what it does and enjoy the things you like about it. Giving away your orgasms in the hope that you won't spill a half-teaspoon of urine doesn't seem like a very good deal to me. Why don't you decide not to do that anymore? Take your orgasm back, take your fifty-five-year-old vagina back, let your husband in on the secret—which probably is no secret to him by now—and enjoy great sex the way you know how." It took a few more sessions of talking, crying, laughing, and learning, but that's just what Camille eventually did: she learned she could wet the bed *and* have great sex.

- Whatever intercourse is like, that's what sex is like.

"Sex hurts, but I guess that's how it sometimes is."

Would you shop in a store that was dirty, had rude personnel, and featured loud, screechy Muzak and disorganized merchandise? Why not? Because like most Americans, you believe you deserve to shop in a place where you can have a good shopping experience. You don't believe you're captive to whatever Macy's or the Gap decides is right; you feel entitled to go to a place where the shopping is comfortable.

If only we felt we deserved as good a sexual experience as we deserve a shopping experience. Then we wouldn't endure painful intercourse for a minute, and would see pain as a clear signal that we need to do a different sexual activity. Instead, we give the ideal of intercourse control over our sexual options, in ways that we wouldn't give away our power to any corporation.

CASE

Pam, Pete, and Pain

"Pam just isn't very interested in sex anymore," said her boyfriend, Pete. "I don't know what to do anymore."

"Neither do I, sweetie," replied the tall, graceful teacher. "I know it's frustrating for you; it is for me, too. That's why we're here."

They were nice people who answered all my questions thoughtfully. I asked about their relationship, communication, how they divided up chores and made decisions. When I started asking about sex they were still thoughtful, although a little shy. We quickly covered subjects like orgasm and masturbation. Then I asked Pam if intercourse was ever painful, and she answered slowly.

"Um, actually, yes, about half the time. Why?" Pete was stunned. "Sex hurts? Since when? Why didn't you tell me?" Pam unfolded the story. "Well, honey, I love you and, um, and, um, well, you know, sex just hurts sometimes." And why hadn't she suggested other sexual activities that might not hurt? "It never occurred to me," said Pam. "I mean, for foreplay they're okay, but it's not like you're going to give up sex just because it hurts."

"I wonder if this accounts for your losing interest in sex," I said simply. "I mean, if you know there's a fifty/fifty chance something will hurt, you wouldn't exactly look forward to it." And that was the start of medical treatment for Pam, as well as a gradual sexual reconciliation of these nice people. By the time they had been sexual together many times with their hands, mouths, and some sex toys, a minor surgical procedure had eliminated Pam's vaginal pain, and they could proceed—slowly, with their new sexual and communication skills—to intercourse. And neither Pam nor Pete called Pam uninterested in sex ever again.

• Sexually competent people prefer intercourse.

"I prefer other kinds of sex, so I must be weird."

Many people enjoy sex but feel apologetic for preferring "foreplay" to "real sex." They fear, in fact, that their preference is unreasonable, and that their partner will judge or resent (even abandon) them because of it. It is so sad that men and women put fences around the unlimited vistas of eroticism. It is so ironic when people feel sad or even angry that sex "can't" be more like what they want—when it already is.

Other people are concerned about not liking intercourse "enough"—that is, getting bored or uncomfortable during prolonged periods of thrusting. This kind of sex requires a strong back, lots of lubrication, periodic attention to the condom if one is being used, and focused concentration. If this is what both partners find delightful, that's great; too often, though, one or both don't, but feel obliged to go ahead anyway, since this is "normal sex." That's a sad mistake.

CASE

Lust or Affection?

Lynn and Morris obviously loved each other, but they just couldn't get on the same sexual wavelength. Morris complained that he wanted more "affection," while Lynn complained that Morris hesitated to open up to his own "lust." We talked at length about what he meant by "affection" and what she meant by "lust." After they went round and round about this for several sessions, I decided to see them each separately.

Morris was obviously nervous at our individual session. With ten minutes to go, I pointed to the clock. "If there's anything you want me to know, Morris, now's the time to tell me," I said. So Morris took a deep breath and told exactly what was on his mind: He secretly wished that most of his sex with Lynn would involve her stroking his penis, playing with his nipples, and giving him fellatio. "In fact," he said, "I fantasize about coming in Lynn's mouth." In our brief time left, I asked Morris to consider telling Lynn some or all of what he had told me. "You don't have to," I said. "But think about how this would change things between you."

Morris rose to the occasion: at our next session he told Lynn practically everything, making it clear that "affection" had been a code word for erotic activities outside of intercourse. "I would do all those things," said Lynn warmly. "I'd love you to ejaculate in my mouth. But you've seemed really uninterested in those things. Why didn't you ever tell me that's what you wanted?" "I didn't want to make it hard for you," Morris told his girlfriend. "I know you like real sex, and I didn't want you to feel you were settling for second best." Needless to say, this was the beginning of several very fruitful conversations. Morris and Lynn are being sexual together regularly—and enjoying it a lot more.

Summary

We've already mentioned how people joke about men being led around by their penises. We observe that men and women are being led around by their penises and vaginas, tied together in culturally required sex: intercourse. How frustrating that people are socialized into a sexual trance, unable to make truly independent sexual choices—which would establish *their own experience* as the fundamental criterion of sexual expression.

In the next chapter we'll look at the challenges and opportunities created by deemphasizing intercourse.

Chapter 4

Can Anyone Enjoy Sex That Isn't "Normal"?

As we have seen, and as you know from personal experience, our society has very strong ideas about how men and women should express their sexuality. Coupled with the centrality of sexuality in most people's lives, this makes eroticism a cornerstone of self-image. Thus, changing the way we think about sex can change the way we think about ourselves, our relationships, and even society. That's why envisioning sex differently presents us with challenges that go way beyond the few hours per week or per month that we make love, and beyond the bedroom altogether.

In this chapter we look at a variety of those challenges, both sexually and nonsexually. These help to explain the hesitation most people have in changing their ideas about sex, the difficulties they encounter when they do, and how sexual changes can lead to nonsexual changes as well. We'll see that the decision to deemphasize intercourse cracks open a whole series of closed doors that have been invisible, raising issues you didn't expect. Handle these challenges well, and many things become possible.

(A) The Challenges Created by Deemphasizing Intercourse

AMBIGUITY

Say you're being sexual with a partner. Is what you're doing "foreplay"? "Real sex"? Will you do it for another twenty seconds, or for a while? How do you know when it's time to move on to something else?

When you don't organize your sexual activity around intercourse, you don't know what any given sexual activity "means." Since you're not fitting sex into the meaning society gives it, your challenge is *to give sex meaning*—a meaning that *you* value. Alternatively, you also have the option of having sex without meaning, just focusing on the experience.

"I feel lost without a reference point or direction" is a common response to deemphasizing intercourse. This speaks to the difference between the two primary ways of thinking about sex. One is holding on to a sense of reality while we dip our toe into sex; the other is letting go of "reality" and floating in eroticism, letting it take us where it may.

When you remove intercourse from the center of your sexuality, you *are* "lost." Can you tolerate the discomfort until you learn to enjoy this perspective? If so, you can explore ways to contain that vertigo, transforming it into a positive feeling and the potential for excitement and enlightenment.

CASE

Manny

"Don't laugh," Manny said at our first session, "but I'm thirty-five years old and I've never had sex with anyone." I'd heard this from dozens of men over the years, but never from someone so handsome, so obviously capable (he was a pharmacist who owned a drugstore), so able to talk about it. Nevertheless, that was the situation.

Manny had a girlfriend, a woman he had dated for years. Although they apparently loved each other, they rarely kissed and had never as much as seen each other nude. "We don't talk about sex," he said simply. "But now we're discussing getting married, and I just have to resolve this sex thing before we do." Manny wanted me to help him get over his "phobia," as he called it, and help him want sex enough to initiate it. "Although Mira hasn't complained, I'm pretty sure she'll go along with it once I'm ready."

"Maybe intercourse isn't what you need right now," I suggested. "There are lots of other things you can enjoy first. In fact, maybe you can let go of the idea of intercourse for a while and be sexual by just exploring each other's bodies in different ways. The variety you'll discover as you two get more and more comfortable will be great."

"No. I mean, I understand we need foreplay to have sex," said the green-eyed, blond man, "but what I'm really concerned about is the sex. If I feel confident I can do that, I'll feel okay about the foreplay. So let's focus on the sex." "You mean the intercourse," I clarified. "Right," said Manny. I tried to explain the flaws in this approach, particularly given his lack of experience. But to my surprise, Manny was adamant. "Don't take it personally," he said, "but I just don't think your concept is for me. I'd be too nervous to do all those things—to talk about our bodies, touch each other's private parts, not know whether or not I would climax, the whole thing sounds just too uncertain. Maybe after I have some experience I can handle this complicated stuff," he said, reaching for his black sport coat, "but this way, it's just too scary for me. I just want to have regular sex with Mira, I want to know what I'm doing and not just—How did you put it?—float in the eroticism, or whatever you said. I'm too nervous to float."

And indeed he was. Our hour was about up, and Manny left quickly. He thanked me for my advice and said he hoped I wasn't angry, but I never saw him again.

STAYING PRESENT WITH YOURSELF

How you actually *feel* becomes a central feature of sex if you're not defining yourself with or worrying about some cultural standard. And that's how you know what to do in bed if you're not following a common sexual script—you each check in with how you feel. But knowing how you feel isn't always easy. In fact, most of us are distracted from our bodies and feelings during sex. Understandably, we feel safer that way.

How does some particular erotic thing feel? Do you like it? What do you want? You may feel nervous considering such questions without the context of normality. It can be even scarier to acknowledge, and accept, the answers.

Many people don't feel much when touched erotically or sensually, or don't enjoy what they do feel. Most of these men and women insist that this is just the way their body is built. The majority, however, do have the capacity to feel and enjoy being touched—when they are relaxed and mentally present. Fear, anxiety, and self-criticism keep us from being present and from feeling how we feel. To some extent, depending on the rules of "normal sex" can cover for your lack of emotional presence during sex. But when you go beyond those rules, all you have left is yourself—if you're there.

YOU MUST COMMUNICATE

An intercourse and "normal" orientation to sex frequently guides people to one of two assumptions: either "we're doing it the 'right way,' so our sex must be (or should be) okay with my partner," or "this isn't the 'normal way,' so my partner probably doesn't like it." When you deemphasize intercourse, however, you can't make these assumptions. To know what's actually going on in bed, you have to communicate with your partner: "Does this feel good?" "What would you like to do now?" "Why did you stop doing that?"

With an outercourse orientation, how you feel physically, emotionally, and spiritually is the central fact of sex at any given moment. Partners create sexual meaning together. If we're not relying on what society says our experience means, we have to communicate this information back and forth to make sense of a sexual encounter. For some people this is an enormous change.

CASE

Sally and Jim

From the very first session, it was clear that Sally and Jim had a good marriage. It reminded me of therapist David Schnarch's comment, that some couples are dissatisfied with marriages that other people would kill for. This marriage did have one big problem: "The sex is mechanical and predictable, and I'm the one who always initiates," according to Sally, a fifty-one-year-old woman with a long, dramatic white ponytail. Her husband, Jim, didn't deny it. "She's right," said the retired airline executive. "I try to change, but sooner or later we slip back into the same routine."

Our initial sessions focused on Sally's anger and Jim's guilt, as well as the positive side of their marriage: cooperative, friendly, enjoyable. "Let's examine how much you bring these strengths into your sexual relationship," I said. "You communicate pretty well about most things, right?" They agreed they did. Money, grandchildren, entertaining, in most things they were usually a good problem-solving team. "As long as I poke Jim every now and then to keep him on a straight path," added Sally with a smile. It was no joke, I said to myself, getting a better and better picture of the complexities of their marriage.

"So let's use those good communication tools you already have," I said cheerfully. "You both agree you'd like variety, especially Sally. So what do you have in mind?" She was suddenly quiet. "Well, are you two interested in oral sex? Masturbating together? What about sex toys, vibrators, videos?" Still no answer. "Hmm," I said gently, "how about if you two talk about this for a few minutes and we'll see if we can get a consensus about where we should head."

But Sally was steaming. "You don't expect me to talk about that stuff, do you?" she demanded angrily. Perhaps I had miscalculated: Was she uncomfortable discussing sex in front of me? "No, not in front of you," she replied, "*anyone,* including Jim. I don't want to talk about sex, and certainly not all that weird stuff. I just want sex to happen. For heaven's sake, is that too much to ask? Jim should lead. Or it should be spontaneous. Look, it's not often, but we do have intercourse—we know what to do, and we do it. Why should we now have to do anything else? And why talk about stuff that's so . . . so rude, so nasty? Vibrators? Yuck, I can't stand talking about that stuff."

As Sally spoke she became increasingly agitated. Clearly, even though she pushed Jim for "better sex," she had a head full of restrictions about it. Outercourse itself violated some of those rules, and the communication that outercourse required violated even more of her rules. "If you want more sexual variety, more communication will be necessary," I said calmly. "One reason you guys are in a rut is because you do only what you already know how to do. Sexual routine is a way of avoiding conflict, surprise, challenge, and having to talk about your experience. If that's your choice, okay, but then don't complain that sex is boring."

Sally transferred a lot of her anger onto me, which was fine, and we spent a number of sessions dealing with that. When we finally resolved much of her anger (and the fear and sadness behind it), she and Jim were able to talk more intimately, and to construct a more fluid, varied, and less predictable sexual relationship. It was confronting what it would mean to expand into outercourse that provided the push that got them there.

QUESTIONING OTHER THINGS

When we remove the arbitrary rules that constitute "normal sex," the question "Why not?" becomes relevant in a surprising number of ways. As a patient once told me, "If it doesn't matter whether it's normal or not, why *not* try toe sucking?" Indeed, why *not* reveal fantasies, or tell stories of old lovers? Why *not* insert your diaphragm in front of your lover, rather than go off to the bathroom? Why *not* admit that your strongest orgasms are from your own hand?

It's an exciting, scary, somewhat disorienting experience to realize that you can create your own experience with far fewer constraints than you once thought necessary. With virtually no external rules to defer to (consent and responsibility, of course, are essential), you're finally in charge of your own sexual expression. This makes the response to many things "Why?" or "Why not?"—which is *not* the way adults are supposed to think about sex in our culture.

Finally, once you deemphasize intercourse, you realize that "sex" is broader than you ever thought possible. Whatever your relationship situation, you suddenly have enormous opportunity to explore your sexuality.

OLD CATEGORIES BECOME OBSOLETE

As victims of the rigid standards of intercourse, most of us, at one time or another, have criticized our sexual selves based on the performance criteria of intercourse. You've probably told yourself, for example, things like "I sporadically lose my erection, therefore . . ."; "My vagina is too loose, therefore . . ."; or "My best orgasms don't come from intercourse, therefore . . ." After a while we tend to think that these categories are who we are, rather than remembering that they are simply maps based on gross approximations. When we tell ourselves stories ("People don't want to give me what I want sexually"; "The sex I like is dirty"; etc.) for a long enough time, we forget that they're just stories.

It's awful feeling inadequate, of course, but at least the old performance standards let us know where we stood. By highlighting our alleged shortcomings, they also provided a supposed explanation for why sex didn't feel the way we wanted it to.

With outercourse, however, you can't be inadequate or defective, since there isn't any defining behavior that makes sex "successful." Thus, you need new categories to describe your experience. You could say you were unimaginative last night, or your body didn't work the way you planned, you two couldn't communicate the way you like, your partner didn't cooperate, you feel disappointed, etc. But you *can't* say that therefore there's something wrong with you, or that because of what you are, sex can't be good. You're forced to use a new (and more complex) vocabulary to describe your experience. That may be uncomfortable at first, even though this vocabulary will inevitably be less harshly self-critical.

With the performance rigidities of intercourse removed, part of our challenge involves facing our own fears about sexuality, the other gender, and intimacy. For example, since the sex doesn't "care" whether you get erect or not, you now have to face why *you* care so much about getting an erection.

GRIEVING FOR LOST OPPORTUNITIES

Reconceptualizing sex is like awakening from a deep sleep. You realize that most of those times when you thought sex was ruined for you, you ruined it yourself; those times when you thought good sex was impossible, you created those limits; and those times when you thought you were sexually inadequate, you simply misunderstood and meanly judged yourself.

Facing the ways in which we've participated in our own deprivation or unhappiness can be so painful, it's tempting to back away from doing so. In fact, the prospect of this pain is the reason some people deny that any other outcome or choices were possible. It takes courage to adopt a sexual perspective (i.e., outercourse) that can, as you're integrating it, make part of your past *more* painful. Learning to grieve for the past without ruining the present is an important life skill.

(B) Opportunities Created by Deemphasizing Intercourse

Those are the challenges—mostly defining sexuality yourself, and staying present enough to direct the experience the way you want it.

What, then, are the payoffs? What opportunities are created

when we meet the challenges to our sense of self and to our long-held assumptions about sexuality, intimacy, and our own adequacy? If changing our ideas about sex creates *challenges* both inside and outside the bedroom, what *opportunities* does it create both inside and outside the bedroom?

NO MORE RECERTIFICATION

"Normality" is always a temporary identity, which has to be continually recertified. But once you accept your own sexuality, the project's over. It's a developmental accomplishment that you get to keep and ultimately ignore, like learning how to drive or getting a high-school diploma.

CASE

Shane the Bus Driver

Shane was one of the nicest guys I ever worked with. He had been sexual with some six or seven women when he came to see me on his fortieth birthday. He had erection problems: "Either I can't get 'em," the bus driver said straightforwardly, "or I get 'em and lose 'em pretty quick. I'm starting to avoid women, which is why I'm here."

Shane was another one of these guys who was devoted to making love the "right way"—and his penis was wilting under the pressure. "I want to be a good lover," Shane told me earnestly. "I want to be a normal guy who does it the normal way. But I can't seem to manage it, which is really tearing at me."

"What about forgetting about doing it right and being normal?"

I asked the surprised Shane. "You're not really paying attention to your partner, and you're certainly not paying attention to yourself. You're off somewhere else, trying to do it right, trying to be normal and a real man and all that, right?" He nodded, fascinated. "Instead, forget about being normal. That's the booby prize. Go and enjoy sex instead. Forget about intercourse"—his eyebrows shot up halfway to the ceiling at this heresy—"and just have a good time. Instead of trying to get your ticket as a good lover punched every time you get into bed, just decide you're going to be Shane every time, instead. That's a guaranteed outcome that you don't have to worry about. And by the way, not that it matters, but your erection will take care of itself."

For some reason, Shane decided that this was the way to go. "Okay, I'll forget about being normal and just have a good time," he said. "And you say the ladies won't mind?" "Not only won't they mind"—I smiled—"but this is exactly what a lot of them are looking for." We met only twice after this, because, as Shane put it, "Since I stopped trying to be normal, my problem's solved!"

SAFER INTROSPECTION

Experimenting with or exploring who you are becomes far less risky (and therefore more likely) because you're not gambling that you'll discover something about yourself or do something that makes you abnormal. Exploring sexuality without the shadow of normality obscuring your vision, you'll simply discover things you like or don't like, things you do or don't want to do again.

This perspective also makes it easier to change your preferences whenever you like, because you can do so without challenging everything you know or believe about sex. You can decide you like anal play after all, without worrying that you're a "latent homosexual." Similarly, you can decide, after years of enjoying it, that you no longer want to hold down your partner during fellatio, regardless of what you think others do.

TOLERATING YOUR PARTNER BETTER

Once you decide that normality isn't an issue for you, it's easy to become less judgmental of your partner's sexuality. That makes it easier to tolerate his/her experimenting: you don't take his/her preferences personally, because you understand they're about your partner's pursuit of his/her own experience.

CASE

Alex—Weirdo or Husband?

Most of his adult life, Alex has fantasized about being held down during sex. His wife, Pam, used to worry about this. "Either he's a weirdo, which isn't okay, or I'm just a stuffy old prude, which isn't okay," the Irish beautician told me at our first meeting. The reasonableness of Alex's fantasies was a recurring source of conflict in their marriage. After only two sessions, I helped them see they were focusing on the wrong thing. "It doesn't matter if what Alex wants is reasonable, or normal, or kinky, or any such judgment," I told them both. "Pam, if you don't want to go along, say 'No, thank you.' Alex, if you're disappointed, say 'Ah, shucks.' Then go and do anything you both agree on doing. Alex, you can have whatever fantasies you like, as long as you respect Pam's limits on your respective behaviors. Pam, you don't have to do anything you don't like, but don't go judging the movies Alex enjoys watching in the privacy of his own head."

We were all pleased at how quickly things worked out. Alex can now ask for, and Pam can now say no to, any sexual requests without creating conflict. In fact, now that Pam spends less time worrying about whether what Alex wants is "normal," she can actually focus on what she *likes* and therefore *wants*—and she's discovering that her tastes are somewhat broader than she thought, because she isn't scared of being a weirdo herself.

THE POINT OF SEX IS CLEARER; SEX BECOMES "JUST SEX"

When sex is not about being normal or adequate, the point of it becomes clearer: experiences like pleasure, surrender, intimacy, and giving. Once sex is closer to "just sex," you can really enjoy it, rather than distracting yourself with questions about performance or perversion.

There are many ways in which a sexual experience can be rich—you may feel intimate, spiritual, graceful—but that will be experiential, not by reference to standards. That is, you wouldn't say "We made love for thirty minutes, *therefore* I'm macho"; rather, you'd say, "Wow, I *feel* so manly right now."

CASE

Stacy—"Not a slut"

"I like sex, but don't get me wrong," the attractive supermarket clerk told me the first time we met, "I'm no slut." Well, I thought, that's clear: she's concerned about the acceptability of her sexuality. I soon found out why. "My older sister was thrown out of the house when I was about twelve," said Stacy in a flat voice. "It didn't matter that she was getting A's in high school. My dad found out she was having sex with her boyfriend, and just threw her out. 'You're just a little tramp,' he said. I remember the scene as if it were yesterday. 'Go find someplace else to live, live with the other tramps and whores.' And then he looked at me—Jesus, I was twelve, I was still getting over the shock of having periods, for God's sake, I didn't understand half of all the commotion—and he said, 'Turn out like that, and you'll be outta here too. Get it?' "

Stacy sure got it, poor thing. Twenty years later, she was still scared of her eroticism. For her, sex still felt like a matter of life and death: a way to lose everything she needed, or a chance to prove she wasn't a slut. Periodically she'd get involved with a man and be sexual, but she worked hard to keep herself under control. She certainly didn't want to do anything wild, which included oral sex, sex with the lights on—anything other than very conventional intercourse. And oh, by the way, "I don't climax like I should," she said, "and it's just impossible to completely relax during sex."

After a couple of sessions we talked about her vague desire to do other sexual things, which conflicted with her conviction that she must not. This was the gateway for our talking about what sex "means," and how she was in fact misusing it. "It seems to me that your sexual difficulties are an understandable consequence of the burden you put on sex," I said. "When you decide that sex can't destroy your life, it will be easier to choose whatever kind of sexual activities you want, and to relax and enjoy them." It took a very long time for Stacy to trust me, herself, and the universe, but after six long months (and the loss of a boyfriend who couldn't stick out the process), Stacy realized that the past was over, and that her sex life today could have no effect on her past. She was then freer to select sexual activities (including masturbation and fantasies) that fulfilled her. She then started to have orgasms periodically. She's now working on increasing their frequency and intensity—by focusing on her experience during sex, rather than judging who she is by what she enjoys.

Sex Presents a Good Oppportunity to Escape from "Normality"

Most people want to feel "normal," and they think of sex as a possible way to establish that feeling. But depending on being sexually "normal" is a burden. You have to follow certain social customs and be concerned about your involuntary reflexes, desires, fantasies, and preferences. Inevitably, you periodically second-guess yourself.

Most important, *no one can be permanently certified* as normal; "normal" is an identity that has to be constantly reaffirmed. In short, *you're only as "normal" as your most recent hour in bed and your last fantasy.*

By definition, this leads to constant insecurity, whether we're conscious of it or not. This ruins sex for a lot of people. It's like a sniffle that never goes away—it's there just enough to keep you from enjoying sex unself-consciously. But we can turn this dilemma inside out—by thinking about sex as a way to *escape* from the burdens of normality.

Once you decide that you can constitute sex as a place with no rules, no goal, and no meaning (other than what you assign it on a given occasion), sex becomes the ultimate escape. Assuming your activity is consensual and nondestructive, you can't do anything wrong, be anything bad, or fail. While you may not have the exact experience you'd like during a particular episode, the result is merely disappointment, not failure or some judgment about you.

This isn't the same as saying "You can escape into the pleasure of sex," although nondestructive pleasure is a very good place to escape to. In the present context, *the pleasure you derive from sex is almost a bonus*: it's lovely and it can even change your life, but it's the non-failure, self-constituted nature of sex that makes it a *real* escape. That's why those for whom sex typically includes a lot of pleasure but also a lot of anxiety don't find sex quite the emotional escape that they might like.

By exploring a sexuality that deemphasizes intercourse and emphasizes personal experience, you can create a mental vacation almost at will. And you can return from it with a better perspective on normality and society's demands. You can reject the need to be normal in any given part of life, based on your experience of enjoying sex despite being non-normal. Or, if you want to, you can actually *choose* the complex goal of normality in some part of life rather than feeling victimized by it.

Using sex to escape from "normality" is a radical move. It says that we're in charge of sex rather than its being in charge of us. It says that escaping from the external pressure to be "normal" is legitimate, not a sign of weakness or immaturity. It says that "using" sex is a reasonable activity, and that affirming one's sense of self is a valid use of sex—that sexuality is ours for the using, rather than our somehow having to serve it.

And, by the way, there is *nothing* wrong with wanting to escape from the burdens of "normality."

(C) What It Takes to Enjoy Sex Outside of the "Normality" Framework

THINK OF "SEXUALITY" IN BROAD TERMS

Deemphasizing intercourse means "sex" doesn't require an orgasm, and there are no tangible criteria for when it's "completed." In fact, sexuality doesn't even necessarily include your penis or vulva. Changing your concept of sex allows you to enjoy it in the moment, rather than continually comparing your experience to some ideal—and, too often, coming up short.

KNOW WHAT YOU WANT FROM SEX

For most men and women, sex is an opportunity to fail. What most people want from sex, therefore, is primarily not to feel bad. As San Francisco sex educator Harvey Caplan, M.D., used to say, "Most people don't want to have big orgies and three-hour orgasms. They simply want to feel okay sexually, not be so embarrassed about how their bodies function, and have their emotional pain taken away."

Emphasizing outercourse eliminates the opportunity to fail in bed. This then creates a question most people have never taken seriously: What do you actually want from sex? Pleasure? Closeness? Experimentation? Giving? Feeling wanted? Most of us aren't honest with ourselves about what we want from sex—partly because we simply don't *know*. As a result, we can't pursue our true sexual desires effectively.

BE ABLE TO CREATE WHAT YOU WANT

Most of us don't have enough knowledge and comfort to feel really confident about our sexual decisions, preferences, and fantasies. This can make non-"normal" sex scary and difficult to create in a relaxed way.

Emphasizing and enjoying outercourse takes trust (in ourselves and our partner), flexibility (staying focused on the erotic when things don't go as planned), and courage (staying open to the emotions that arise during intense, unprogrammed sex). What else do you need to create the sex you want? An acceptance of your own aggressive instincts? Approval of your desire to be cuddled, or your desire for endless passionate kissing? Do you have the information you need? about the G-spot? The effects of medications on your sexuality? The secrets of Tantric sex? Whether or not pornography is "dangerous"?

Whatever information, technical skill, and emotional tools you need to create open-ended sex, acquire them. Resources include books, Web sites, and professionals such as sex therapists and nurses. The Appendix is a good place to start.

VALIDATE YOURSELF

Understandably, most of us turn to the reassurance of being "normal" when we feel insecure or unsure of ourselves. In order really to thrive with outercourse, however, you need to be able to soothe yourself and do without that validation. It also helps to be part of a community in which you feel validated; ways of doing this include reading, friendships, and a spiritual tradition. You can even assemble a community mentally, without the other "citizens" knowing. An example of this is divorced Catholics who use Jesus' teachings to justify their entitlement to love and support, even though the Church itself doesn't approve.

TELL YOURSELF A MEANINGFUL STORY

Under the "normal sex"/intercourse regime, when you and your partner stroke each other and get excited, you know what you're doing: "foreplay." In the outercourse model, however, you *don't know* what you're doing. It could be playing, it could be arousing each other, it could be stimulating one or both of you to orgasm, or even something else. Multiply this by the various sexual feelings, thoughts, and experiences you have in, say, a year, and that's a lot of not knowing. There's nothing wrong with that—it's actually very exciting—although it's nice to have a broad narrative to hold it all together. Learn to describe your (new) sexual style to yourself, which will help you tolerate the ambiguity of any given erotic moment. For example, you might tell yourself "Well, women's magazines never discuss older women using vibrators; I guess I'm a little adventurous and they're a little cowardly; how lucky to be a pioneer!"

If you feel particularly connected to one or another social institution whose norms you're breaking (e.g., your religion or your family or *Ladies' Home Journal*), it also helps to construct a story to make this behavior meaningful to yourself. That is, instead of feeling bound by the traditional definitions of institutions as others understand them, take a proactive position in *defining* institutions for *yourself*.

For example, you might decide that God doesn't care what part of your body you put into what part of your partner's body, and that the Church's position on things like anal sex is simply misinformed. This has been the strategy, for example, of many gays who are Catholic and who want to feel a part of the Church.

We now turn to Part II, in which we explore the nuts and bolts of outercourse. Here's where you implement your decision to deemphasize intercourse and explore the rich world of an alternative sexual universe.

Part II

Beyond "Normal Sex"

Chapter 5

What Is Outer-course?

Outercourse is the word we use to describe both a set of erotic behaviors and an attitude toward them. We contrast it with *intercourse,* which supposedly describes a simple set of behaviors but that, for most people today, really includes an entire approach to sex, a set of norms and expectations, a feeling of pressure, and the resulting self-criticism.

So outercourse is more than what you do with your body; the sexual perspective is crucial. It's possible to have non-intercourse sex in ways that you fill with pressure and expectations, making it like the kind of intercourse we're trying to get you away from. And, as we'll see in chapter 7, it's also possible to integrate the self-affirming attitudes of outercourse into your intercourse.

Outercourse can be both genital and nongenital. For example, we insist that there's no such thing as "erogenous zones." Every part of your body is an erotic zone; the question is which ones you've awakened. It's like getting a new credit card in the mail, which you have to activate by calling a special number: if you don't call, the credit line is unusable. Well, the various parts of your erotic body don't feel much if you haven't activated them.

The concept of outercourse avoids judgments about what is or isn't a "sexual" part of the body. Similarly, it challenges the idea that some erotic things are sexual and others aren't. You've probably already felt this yourself. Haven't you ever thought that someone's self-confidence, or competence, or compassion was sexy?

That said, we know that certain parts of the body are loaded with nerve endings, including the mouth, anus, genitals, and hands. Outercourse invites you to combine these body parts in new ways, so go ahead and experiment: mouth on nipple, teeth on toe, finger in anus, tongue in back of the knee.

Outercourse involves a vision of your own eroticism that you design and control. This erotic vision is not subject to the whims of biology, aging, or social custom. It isn't static; you can alter it as you mature, change partners, cope with physical limitations, or grapple with life issues like boredom, fear of aging, and the empty-nest syndrome.

This outercourse vision has a radical absence of rules (other than consent, honesty, and responsibility): about how bodies should function, about who does what, about how long you should spend doing various activities, about what anything "means." How, then, do you evaluate various erotic events? By referring to your own experience, not to ideas about how bodies are supposed to function during sex. That is, by how you *feel,* not by what you *think.*

Because outercourse doesn't involve the rules and expectations that so easily create performance pressure, it contains the strong potential for playfulness. After all, when your only goals are pleasure or closeness, and whatever your body does is okay, and you're naked and relaxed with someone you like, being playful is not difficult. For the same reason, outercourse offers a particularly good chance to experiment with eroticism.

Similarly, another hallmark of outercourse is connectedness. Without the distraction of expectations and the fear of failing, you can actually pay attention to where you are and whom you're with. And that's when people can feel connected to each other. Another type of connectedness is spirituality, which you are also freer to experience when you don't care how your body is performing.

While everyone talks about desire for and arousal before sex, few people talk about desire and arousal *during* sex. It can be a challenge to maintain psychological and physical interest in sex that is routine, no matter how you feel about your partner. The outercourse approach addresses this need: try changing the location or time of day of your sexual encounters; change the order of what you usually do, and change the lighting—turn the lights on if they're usually off, and vice versa.

You'll find us repeating various descriptions of outercourse in the chapters of Part II. When attempting to change decades of thinking, and centuries of cultural beliefs, there's no such thing as too much repetition.

What to Do

Just for fun, here's a list—in no particular order—of outercourse activities that different people enjoy. Remember, a self-accepting, nonpressured attitude makes all the difference.

- Kiss: particularly, as actor Kevin Costner said in the film *Bull Durham,* with "slow, wet kisses that last two days." Or kiss every part of your partner's body *except* his/her mouth.
- Masturbate: while your partner watches, or simultaneously.
- Masturbate each other. Maintaining eye contact while doing so greatly increases the intensity and intimacy.
- Watch dance shows on TV without the sound.
- Oral sex: the stimulation of your mouth by your partner's genitals (and vice versa). Don't rush, don't try to do it perfectly, and don't stretch your body in ways it doesn't want to go. Then enjoy the taste, smell, and intimacy. If either of you is squeamish, bathe—together—first. Don't know what your partner likes? Ask for a demonstration on a piece of fruit.
- When your partner's really excited, sprinkle him/her with water or ice.
- Anal stimulation: either around the outside, or into the passageway itself; with finger, object, or penis. Remember to go slowly, relax, and use lubrication.
- Dominance and submission: holding your partner down, being held down, using a blindfold, spanking, using wrist or ankle restraints; playact at "forcing" someone to do something.

Remember, this is very intimate stuff, so clear communication is essential.

- Phone sex: with a lover or stranger, or sharing a commercial service with your partner. You can touch yourself while talking and listening, or do so after you hang up. You can drive someone wild by telling a story, saying what you'd do if you were there, or pretending you already are.
- Cuddle as if you've never done it before, and discover what it feels like.
- Massage.
- Erotic massage.
- Vibrators: for both men and women, in or on virtually any part of the body. No, you won't get "addicted."
- Play with the shower massager.
- Nipple stimulation: with finger, mouth, teeth, vibrator, and different temperatures. You can pull, squeeze, twist, pinch, push, and torment, as well as nibble, bite, chew, lick, suck, tease, and taste. Remember that the more excited someone is to start with, the more stimulation s/he can enjoy—and that talking and eye contact also help your partner tolerate higher intensities.
- Put your finger in your partner's vagina and explore what it's really like in there. Find out what she likes best.
- Play with textures: feathers, leather, virtually anything.
- Play with oil or lotion, either with your hands, or by sliding the two bodies over each other.
- Exhibitionism: show off with your mate, go out without underwear, grope your partner in public, hope you get caught doing something erotic, "accidentally" flash a sexy part of your anatomy, discuss the sex you had (or will have) when others can hear.

- Shower together.
- Feed each other with fingers.
- Fantasy: There's literally no limit to what you can imagine, or how you can add it to your sexplay. You can role-play scenes: the pirate and the helpless maiden, the priest and the prostitute, the last two people on earth, etc. You can pretend there's a third person in bed with you, and talk about what s/he's doing; you can pretend you're being watched by someone in the bedroom; you can even go separately to a bar, and "meet" each other and have a one-night stand.
- Arrange to be watched while having sex.
- Dance or strip for your lover.
- Use pornography: read to each other, act out scenes you read or see, describe to each other what you're watching.
- Take photos or make audio- or videotapes of your lover or yourself.
- Dress up fancy for no reason, and ask your partner to undress you.

We're confident you can discover many more erotic adventures once you let go of restrictive ideas like "normal sex," "doing it," and "erogenous zones." Are the activities listed above "sex"? We think there are better questions to ask: Does it feel good? Make me glad I have a body? Allow me to enjoy myself with less performance anxiety? Nourish my connection with my partner?

When it comes to eroticism and sexual satisfaction, these are the questions to ask. And outercourse is a powerful answer.

Chapter 6

Advantages of Outercourse

We have now looked at "normal sex" and intercourse, our attachment to both, and the results. We've defined outercourse as a state of mind, and given lots of examples. Now it's time to examine outercourse more closely, and see the wide variety of advantages it offers. This chapter focuses on why we *need* outercourse, particularly at this stage of human evolution.

Many events and transitions have shaped the development of human sexuality. The following events trace *the evolution of sexual intercourse* in Western culture summarized in roughly chronological order.

As mammals, our ancestors adapted to changing environmental conditions and evolutionary pressures. Human females gradually *lost the recurring period of estrus,* or sexual receptivity ("being in heat"), that most mammals still have. This meant that humans were able to be sexual together all month long, throughout whatever relationship they chose to have. At about the same time, evolutionary changes in our ancestors' bodies (skeletons, penis size, vaginal musculature) made *face-to-face intercourse possible,* and rear-entry intercourse more difficult. Each of these changes was a significant step forward in emotional contact and pair bonding, with all its implications.

Eventually, humans learned to herd animals, to farm, and to create cities. To support these activities, people wanted to influence nature, and so they developed complicated behaviors designed to do so. Thus, in many parts of the world, *cult prostitution* and *ritual (male) homosexuality* became "normal." In the Bronze Age and biblical era, *polygamy* was considered "normal," although by the early Middle Ages *monogamy* had become far more common, and *heterosexuality* was the norm. The first few centuries after Jesus also saw the development of a new norm: that sex is *bad, dirty, and destructive.*

The Industrial Age also created a *sexualized culture,* with advertising and mass media, and medical, religious, and legal obsessions with sexuality. Although *contraception* had been attempted for millennia (the ancient Egyptians used crocodile dung), more dependable herbal remedies, various devices, and finally condoms and birth control pills became widely available. As life expectancy increased, and marginalized groups gained sexual consciousness and political power, the number of *people expecting to enjoy intercourse increased greatly*. And in this very century, the newest wide-scale sexual norm of all unfolded: that *people should want intimacy from sex*.

Thus, the framework for typical human sexual experiences has changed dramatically over time. People rarely consider this, generally assuming that our bodies and our sexuality have been stable throughout human history. The very fact of this evolution can help us accept the challenging notion of sexuality as arbitrary and constructed.

The first era described above was tens of thousands of years long; the second era, many thousands; and the third only a few hundred. This reflects the increased pace of change in human culture and human life, for better or worse. Humans' increasing ability to modify their sexual environment—surgical sterilization, sex-reassignment surgery, and cyber-sex, to name just a few—is truly breathtaking. Humans will undoubtedly continue to create new landscapes in which future humans will be sexual. Today we humans can—and should—change our sexual behavior and beliefs in response to changes in our physical and emotional environment.

As human sexual culture changes, the psychological context of its components—desire, behavior, and experience—keeps changing too. *What people want from sex* has also changed and now includes extraordinarily *modern* things, some of which you probably want, too. The change in what we want from sex requires a change in the way we have sex—and that means outercourse.

What many people now want from sex includes:

- **More intimacy**: Westerners today face new existential issues like nuclear war and the collapse of the traditional family. One-to-one intimacy (including sexual intimacy) has never been more praised or sought after. Nineteenth- and twentieth-century romantic art (both high and popular culture) tells us this profound intimacy is both desirable and possible.

• **Eroticism despite physical limitations:** Our sexual reflexes and hormone levels begin to ebb after age thirty-five—which used to be the average human life expectancy. In addition, an enormous range of modern medications undermine sexual expression. Finally, people with health problems such as diabetes and hypertension now expect life to include sexual satisfaction.

Pain, either specifically sexual or chronic and nonsexual, creates special challenges. In days gone by, people for whom intercourse was physically painful were expected either to suffer with it and do their duty, or withdraw from sex altogether (often without explaining why). In today's culture, more and more people with various painful health conditions are demanding the right to be sexual, and so they need alternatives to intercourse. These health issues range from sexual pain (dyspareunia, vaginismus, etc.) to nonsexual pain (arthritis, fibromyalgia, etc.).

• **Self-exploration and expression:** God has been pushed aside in many bedrooms; people have changed from "sex is a duty" to "sex is for satisfaction"; and Western philosophy emphasizes the individual. Thus, the *self* has become a key player in sexual expression for the first time. Correspondingly, people increasingly look to sex as a vehicle for exploring and expressing themselves. Sex has become, variously, an art form, a recreational sport, a way of expressing emotion, and a format for discovering oneself, both for people in relationships and for people in between relationships.

To put it another way, now that the self is legitimized as a big part of sexual experience, sex can be used to explore or express that self. This is best said by the Italian maxim that translates to "Bed is the poor man's opera."

• **Dealing with a sexualized environment:** In twentieth-century Western culture, sexual images are used to portray an almost infinite variety of things, such as emotions, status, energy, character, and achievement. Dealing with this continual, subliminal pressure is actually a new human chore; people are still developing coping strategies in order to thrive erotically in this environment so full of unrealistic images and contrived urgency.

• **The desire for satisfaction within long-term relationships, and for the elderly:** Longer life spans now create couples that are together for thirty, forty, and fifty years. At the same time, an increasing number of older people expect to be fully sexual. Thus, forms of sexual expression that work for older people who have grown accustomed to each other are needed.

Older people, of course, used to be a tiny minority in every society. Those who were alive knew they were considered disqualified from sex, and few attempted to challenge this publicly. Now things are different. Older men and women are beginning to believe that they deserve sex if they want it. But as Stanford University gerontologist Dr. Walter Bortz notes, the single biggest obstacle is men's "potency." While this is factually correct as far as it goes, putting it this way obscures the real issue: older couples, like everyone else, think that sex is intercourse. Remove that belief, and all those nonerect penises become nonproblematic. That's what modern older people need—a new way to think about sex, so that they can be sexual regardless of physical capacity.

• **Sex without fear of HIV:** Although people have attempted to avoid STDs for thousands of years, HIV (the virus that causes AIDS) is a very special modern plague. More people are infected worldwide today than all the people in history before 1945 combined who got STDs. And, experimental (and extremely expensive) drugs notwithstanding, it is a virtual death sentence for most people who get it.

Here in the United States, millions of people suffer from EFRAIDS: Exaggerated Fear Reaction to AIDS. Their fear has rendered them almost phobic about intercourse, which is exacerbated by the disinformation being spread about condoms by groups trying to prevent "immorality" and teenage sex. While outercourse doesn't totally prevent AIDS, it can (except for unprotected anal intercourse) greatly reduce the chance of getting it.

- **Sex that doesn't risk pregnancy**: American youth are notorious for two aspects of their sexuality: They have sex at very young ages, and they rarely use condoms. Many government and private campaigns try to reduce teen pregnancy by preaching abstention from "sex." But for most teens, this is simply not feasible. Instead, teen sexuality needs to be redirected to outercourse. Properly conceived, this activity could satisfy young people without creating so many unwanted pregnancies.

The ways in which humans have been having sex for tens of thousands of years cannot completely address these new needs and psycho-erotic realities. *Thus, we need new forms of sexual relating*. But most people don't think of this possibility, because we think of sexuality and gender as given (by God or nature), rather than as negotiable. Once you think of eroticism as constructed, and see sexual norms as arbitrary, it is easier to imagine adapting sexuality to a changing human culture. This would be similar to the way we continue to adapt our ways of childrearing (rethinking spanking) and eating (reducing fat intake) to a changing physical and psychological environment.

The lack of agreement about norms, the culture wars focusing on erotic expression, the lack of agreement on who is a sex expert, the conflicts over eroticism in established fields like medicine, law, religion, and psychology, all make it clear that *we are living through an era of evolutionary change with regard to sexuality.*

So what might new forms of sexual relating look like? In addition to addressing our contemporary needs (e.g., novelty, security) ,we'd want them to consider human limitations (e.g., jealousy). Note that our needs and desires may be internally contradictory (e.g., novelty vs. security), which can make erotic exploration emotionally painful. Finally, we might want these new forms to address aspects of eroticism that are now underdiscussed, such as spirituality, power, and modern psychological issues such as the desire to feel competent and the desire to feel known.

Our exploration of "outercourse" is the opening shot in a long-term process of remodeling sexual norms and exploring sexual options. In terms of human development, it comes along with other contemporary developments such as reliable contraception and the extended physical and psychological longevity that allows older people to be sexual. Naturally, this book cannot resolve all the issues of contemporary eroticism; in fact, knowing that this is a work in progress makes it easier to accept that we're not going to get it all perfect.

Some of the other things this long-term project will explore include the nature of sexual attraction and desire; the phenomenon of jealousy; appropriate forms of adolescent sexual expression; and the intersection of lust and spirituality. Yes, this is definitely a long-term project, one that advances in psychology and medicine have now made possible.

Outercourse as Non-"Normal" Sex

By definition, *"normal"* refers to standards shaped by long-standing, conventional needs and approved of by society's power structure. For example, the Western psycho-social "need" to procreate and the Western idea that sex is primarily for the young and able-bodied are both over a thousand years old.

So one reason that the sexual expression evolving in response to newly developing human needs *can't* be "normal" is that it's so new. Outercourse also can't be "normal" because it is so personal; individuals make it up as they go along, rather than referring to a "right" way of doing things.

Just for the sake of argument, let's assume that a lot of people acting independently all create outercourse that looks identical. While this format would then be *statistically* normal, it wouldn't be *subjectively* "normal" because each person would have created it from scratch rather than by adopting existing models. Indeed, although their sex lives would not be uncommon, many of these people might still feel like renegades because they would have constructed their sexuality without reference to current norms. The 1960s are a good example of this. Millions of young people were expressing their sexuality in similar ways, but most felt like rebels because they were specifically flouting contemporary social standards.

Because outercourse isn't "normal," it offers many opportunities. Through it, we can experience ourselves functioning outside social norms—and surviving. We can grow by seizing the chance to validate *ourselves,* rather than relying on others to do it for us. And we can make sexual decisions based on our own experience, rather than by reference to norms or what we imagine others want or think.

Ultimately, outercourse is the vehicle for humans writing a new sexual narrative. This is the ultimate opportunity that we get from outercourse.

The very idea of an arbitrary, constructed sexual narrative is quite modern. For millennia, people have sought to find out what the gods or God "wanted" regarding their sexuality. The answers they ascertained have varied widely across cultures, from the total asexuality of Augustine to the total eroticism of Rajneesh. Other people, such as the ancient Greeks and modern American Religious Right, have earnestly speculated about "natural" sexuality—something wired into our bodies or souls. This belief in a "natural" sexuality is the basis for condemning women's sexual equality, and for criminalizing homosexual and other victimless sexual behaviors as "crimes against nature."

Many of those who recognize the chance to write their own sexual narrative are already involved in one or another minority culture. This outsider's perspective, with its own norms and vocabulary, creates a special vantage point from which to view mainstream culture and its constraints—as arbitrary creations of fallible humans. Such subcultures include those centering on homosexuality, S/M, recreational drugs, and the arts. To marginalized subcultures having to re-create their own norms every day, writing a sexual narrative makes intuitive sense.

Once we realize that there's a sexual narrative to write (or rewrite), we have the extraordinary opportunity of doing so consciously. It's a chance to align your personal impulses, decisions, and experiences with a new, personally created "norm." It's a chance to create a conceptual vocabulary that can fit with your experiences, rather than attempting to fit your unique experiences into an off-the-rack linguistic and conceptual vocabulary that may fit poorly or not at all. This, after all, is one of the things that make people crazy—having experiences that mainstream culture cannot adequately describe, and therefore deems impossible or wrong.

It's a scary opportunity, because you create a situation in which you're out on a limb. Like a mechanical crane that builds a skyscraper by continually re-creating itself on the newly uppermost floor, you literally create norms *after* your experience; you create a vocabulary to describe your unique experience and then declare it meaningful. You become, in essence, a culture of one—mainstream to yourself.

Because you've done it yourself, you know that your beliefs are merely created, not "true" in any sense. This helps keep you from taking them too seriously. Ultimately, then, you can only fall back on the integrity of your own experience and intention, because you know there is nothing more. Imagine being mentally strong enough to do that. And imagine the payoff—you become the center of your own erotic world, with the option of accessing 100 percent of your own erotic energy. This is far better than having a big portion of it siphoned off by issues of "normality"—it's like owning a home rather than renting.

Doing this requires different skills than those of lovemaking per se. It requires tolerance of ambiguity, lack of the need for authority figures, a sense of humor, and a willingness to face the truth about your own eroticism (such as your desires and preferences). Although periodically this is hard on the nerves, you get something marvelous in return.

Details of Outercourse

It can be hard to see the advantages of outercourse from the perspective of the old intercourse-oriented paradigm. Remember, this involves rearranging your thinking, not just your body parts.

In every known society, socially competent adults know which sexual behaviors are and aren't acceptable. Even more important, they know that *some* sexual activities are considered wrong, immoral, dangerous, unacceptable, *even when done by consenting adults in private.* A modern outercourse-oriented sexuality asserts just the opposite: *Any mutually consenting, responsible erotic behavior is acceptable.*

Such an assertion is serious business. Deciding that anything consensual is possible alters one's mind permanently by throwing *all* social norms into question. "If I can manage sexual behavior X, maybe taboo sexual behavior Y is okay, too," a person might speculate. Another might think, "If my church has misled me about sexual expression X, what else might they be wrong about?"

America was rocked by such sincere skepticism some thirty years ago. When young people discovered that the government lied about both recreational drugs and the extent of the Vietnam War, many became skeptical about *all* social norms and assumptions. Many people who now experiment successfully with sexuality—by playing with S/M, bisexuality, or open relationships, for example—are going through a similar disorientation, and are finding themselves moving toward the fringe of society in nonsexual areas as well. In general, questioning social norms can be a powerful and productive thing. Almost everyone can handle the consequences of what they discover when they experiment with their own sexuality in a responsible way.

Outercourse is about people tailoring sex to their own unique needs and desires. The result will be different for different people, emphasizing different blends of pleasure, safety, and intimacy. Personalizing your sexual expression in this way requires a belief in your own entitlement—that creating the sex you want is not too much to ask for, that it won't disrupt "the mood" with someone, that what you want is reasonable.

Largely because of our emphasis on intercourse, Westerners overfocus on their genitals during sex, to the detriment of the other two thousand square inches of skin and the five physical senses. Through these senses we enjoy our partners' smell, taste their mouth, skin, and genitals, admire the graceful lines of their body, get aroused by the squishing sound of erotic moisture. Rigid social norms about "proper" forms of sexual expression trample on these sensual opportunities. Outercourse is a way of highlighting, multiplying, and devouring these erotic experiences.

Outercourse has the potential to change the basis of erotic connecting, *from performance to presence*. We look at erotic presence in more detail in chapter 7, but first let's examine the issue of erotic connection.

Most people say they want to connect with their sexual partner(s) and to "feel close" during and after sex. What exactly do people mean by that? What do *you* mean by that? To various people it means:

sharing each other's experience
feeling permission to do or say anything
feeling accepted

feeling comfortable about your body
feeling confident about being easily understood
having access to a partner's body, thoughts, and feelings
feeling that you really know your partner
tolerating mistakes, disappointment, and misunderstanding
expecting to be treated nicely

Outercourse is an *excellent* facilitator of all of these. With its reduced performance focus, emphasis on sensuality, and individual construction, it offers the communication and self-awareness that can help partners feel really close.

Outercourse has a complex relationship with traditional Eastern practices such as Tantra. On the one hand, Eastern disciplines do focus on sensuality and other aspects of outercourse such as breathing, eye contact, and slow, relaxed motions. On the other hand, Tantra and other traditions typically talk about intercourse as being the centerpiece of a couple's sexual union. This is unnecessarily rigid and may have developed because of the strict sex roles found in almost all ancient traditions. In truth, the conscious penis-vagina intertwining that these disciplines teach is about as far from the frenzied, unconscious "screwing" of many modern Americans as you can get, proving that outercourse is a state of mind, not a fixed set of activities.

Finally, let's examine some specific, tangible *advantages of outercourse*.

Perhaps the most obvious is the *virtual impossibility of pregnancy*. Whether two partners are against abortion, or they're too young to parent, or they hate using condoms, or birth control pills are ruled out for health reasons, or they simply want a sexual environment with no risk of conception, outercourse is the way to go.

People have been using oral and anal sex for precisely this reason for centuries; the term "technical virgin"—meaning someone who has had a penis inside her, but not in her vagina—has a long history.

Similarly, outercourse is one way to *control exposure to STDs*. It's not perfect by any means—people get herpes from oral sex and AIDS from anal sex—but there are ways to reduce the risk of getting these, and there are many satisfying forms of outercourse for which there is NO risk of either. In many ways, outercourse can be a middle ground between risk and abstinence.

Outercourse is *inclusive*: it's available to everyone, regardless of age, ableness, health difficulties, etc. No erection? No problem. Back hurt, knees hurt, hips hurt? No problem. Allergic to latex or spermicides? No problem. If you want to be sexual and you're interested in outercourse, nothing need stand in your way.

We have already seen how outercourse enables us to *honor the senses* more than most people do during intercourse. It greatly reduces the occurrence and fear of rapid ejaculation, which is a blessing for many couples. By giving people permission to focus on exactly whatever they enjoy (kissing, caressing, oral sex, whatever), it inevitably slows people down during sex. When you're doing something you enjoy, you don't worry that things are taking too long. And the essential unpredictability of outercourse can enhance novelty, because there's no script to follow.

At the same time, outercourse also *facilitates orgasm*. It is well documented that most American women cannot orgasm from intercourse alone; a quick look at the geography of the vagina (where the penis goes) and clitoris (where stimulation typically triggers orgasm) explains why. What is less well known is that many men have difficulty climaxing from intercourse alone, especially after age forty. A mouth or hand (his partner's or his own) can frequently provide the exact stimulation a man needs better than a vagina can. It's also far easier to instruct a partner in how to move his/her hand or mouth than in how to move a penis or vagina during intercourse.

One of the best things about outercourse is the way it can *reduce performance pressure,* because there are no expectations, requirements, or standards for "success." Of course, people can add these things to outercourse—e.g., needing him to maintain an erection for a specified length of time, or needing her to orgasm within a certain period of time—but it takes effort to do so, as most people intuitively give themselves (and their partners) more slack with outercourse than they do with intercourse. In particular, erections are not necessary for satisfying outercourse. This can provide great relief for people who worry about this. In fact, sex therapists routinely prohibit intercourse for a month or two for patients who obsess about getting or maintaining an erection.

What About Viagra?

You've undoubtedly heard about Viagra, Pfizer's drug for erectile dysfunction. Physicians across America are prescribing it at the drop of a, um, penis. Several similar drugs will be appearing in the next eighteen months as well.

Viagra promises that men who take it *under the right conditions* will get erect with a minimum of stimulation. While this may seem like a pretty good deal, it's a lot more complicated than it sounds. We're not just talking about possible side effects; we're talking about the consequences of the drug working exactly the way it's intended to.

WHY PEOPLE TAKE IT

Tens of thousands of men are now taking Viagra to get erections so they can have intercourse.

Men are also taking the drug for other reasons. For example, some are taking it to feel more confident, even though they have rarely or never had an erection problem. Some men take the drug because their partners push them to do so—whether in response to true erectile difficulty or simply to reduce the partner's anxiety. Some men take the drug because they don't have the emotional or communication skills to handle the occasional lack of erection, or to enjoy non-intercourse sex. And some men take it because they think it will enhance their desire for sex with their mate.

We think that these are all issues that men would be better off facing, rather than medicating away. We believe that anxiety, lack of skills, and relationship problems are better dealt with than ignored or covered over.

Our combined forty years' experience in answering people's questions also makes it clear that many men and women find intercourse overrated as a source of pleasure. They enjoy other kinds of eroticism—cunnilingus, kissing, and masturbating together, just to name a few—as much as or more than intercourse. Thus, taking a drug simply to facilitate intercourse seems a poor strategy for enhancing erotic satisfaction.

WHAT IT DOES

After a man has taken Viagra (assuming he has no physical difficulties such as advanced diabetes), direct physical stimulation will produce an erection unless a very strong emotion gets in the way. Such emotions include anxiety, anger, and fear. Thus, Viagra will sometimes reveal a man's emotional state, of which his partner or even he has been unaware.

Furthermore, Viagra will make a man *erect, not excited*—a crucial distinction. Most men have had the experience of being erect because they have to urinate, or upon awakening from a sexy dream, or when embarrassed during a doctor's examination. None of these is the same as being sexually aroused. A man taking Viagra may not be mentally excited, even though his penis is erect, and he may therefore need additional mental or physical stimulation to be interested in sex. When mates don't feel friendly, or they don't communicate well, this need for additional touching or talking may be more than they bargained for.

WHAT IT DOESN'T DO

As we have noted, Viagra does not create mental excitement, only physical arousal. Further, except insofar as getting an erection can be sexy for some men, it does not create desire. A man without erections who doesn't desire his wife and who takes Viagra will typically become a man *with* erections who doesn't desire his wife. In this case, Viagra will again reveal something about a man's inner being that he may not be aware of, or may not wish to expose.

Taking this one step further, a woman who is angry at her mate's bossiness or refusal to listen before he takes Viagra will generally feel the same way after he takes it. She may feel his lack of erection is a minor issue compared to others.

Viagra does not enhance communication (nor does it claim to). This is important, because far more sexual relationships are limited, disrupted, or destroyed by poor communication than by poor erections.

UNANTICIPATED CONSEQUENCES

Various clinical trials suggest that Viagra works in only about two-thirds of the men who take it.

But we are particularly concerned about the unintended impact of this drug *when it works exactly as promised*. A lot can go wrong with a store-bought erection: not with the erection itself but with the person to whom it is attached, and with the relationship in which it's used.

We can easily imagine a woman looking at her partner's nice, shiny erection and wondering, "Is it me or is it the drug?" For many women this will be troublesome; for insecure women, it will be a nightmare. Of course, women should not base their sense of adequacy on their partner's erection, but many do.

Another reaction some women will have to Viagra is accusing their mates of infidelity. "When he couldn't have sex [meaning intercourse], I didn't worry," wives across America will think. "Now that he can do it whenever he wants to, I bet he will—and not just with me." Soon we'll hear stories about suspicious women catching their mates cheating by counting pills: "There were twelve here last month. There are eight now, and we've only made love once. Where have you used the others?"

Another common story will be women pushing their mates for more sex than the mates want. "You have no excuse now," some wives will say. "C'mon, Buster."

Of course, various men will have their own reactions. Some will respond with a burst of sexual interest, chasing their partners around the house to use their new toy more often than the relationship can support. After six years of no erections, introducing erections on demand without any psychological preparation will be disruptive.

Some men will begin (or resume) having extramarital affairs, now that they feel they can. No one actually knows how many men don't have affairs simply because they're embarrassed to reveal their erection difficulties.

Men will have their own existential questions: What, now, makes me a man? What exactly am I needed for in a sexual situation? Am I any different than a dildo with a credit card?

Finally, it will be interesting to see how many relationships suffer a decrease in the amount of kissing, oral sex, and other nonintercourse behaviors when people can have erections on demand.

SUMMING UP

We believe that America's search for a Viagra-like pill (and the extraordinary celebration at its commercial release last spring) is one more reflection of our culture's limited perspective on sexuality.

Of course it's great to have (medical) solutions to medical problems. But a great deal of erection problems are either a) a penis responding appropriately to a situation of relationship turmoil, emotional conflict, alcohol abuse, or inadequate stimulation; or b) a developmental challenge of aging that is as much an opportunity as a problem.

These may look like erection problems, but they aren't. Viagra won't fix these types of situations; it will allow people to bypass these issues, inviting future problems and exacerbating real non-sexual ones. We fear that many couples will be using Viagra to avoid uncomfortable but necessary conversations.

The new erection pill is a perfect representative of our uniquely tormented time: it can provide ability without feelings, orgasm without joy, virility without connection. We think drugs like Viagra are wonderful for certain people—particularly older people with slight nerve or vascular problems. (We still advocate that these people rev up their communication and intimacy skills to best take advantage of Viagra.) For everyone else, we advocate old-fashioned personal and couples growth. As we say many times throughout this book, this will either facilitate erections, or allow people to enjoy sex without them.

Chapter 7

Beyond "Foreplay," Beyond Intercourse

"Foreplay" refers to erotic activities before and preparatory to intercourse. For various people this involves kissing, caressing, affectionate whispers, and different kinds of genital play. The word *foreplay* divides the entire world of amorous activities into "before intercourse" and "during intercourse." This division is neither "natural" nor "real"; if people don't proceed to intercourse (either because they didn't intend to, were distracted by other pleasurable things, climaxed, or changed their minds), the distinction collapses altogether.

For many people foreplay has become a chore before the fun, like waterproofing your ski boots or waxing your surfboard before you go out and enjoy yourself. Responses to having to do this chore range among resentment, resignation, shrugging acceptance, and defensiveness.

Once you deemphasize intercourse, however, you don't "have" to do "foreplay"; rather, you simply have a large set of erotic behaviors from which to choose, and you can select at whim and continue purely on the basis of whether or not you enjoy them. Activities known as "foreplay" can be completely enjoyable when they're not "foreplay."

This book proposes eliminating the concept of "stuff you have to do in preparation for something else" and instead suggests that you describe various erotic activities as just that. Rather than categorizing erotic experiences based on their position in a sequence of activities, you can take the radical step of *eliminating the sequence*. After all, once the erotic energy begins to flow, you're *already* someplace special. Without intercourse providing the context for everything else, nothing is "preparation"; it's all simply experience.

This frees you to do only things you enjoy, in whatever order you want. You can then enjoy each sexual moment and activity without regard to what it "accomplishes." Put another way, there's no reason to do anything sexually that you don't want to, because nothing is preparing or accomplishing anything. And since there's no goal, there can be no "performance," only experience. So, within the values of consent and honesty, how something feels—the moment-to-moment erotic experience—is all that matters. That's the best way to evaluate what you're doing in bed—how it *feels*.

CASE

John and Sharon: ". . . when we remember to have it!"

John's wife was always happy to share fellatio with him when they were sexual together. Not only did Sharon like giving John pleasure, she also enjoyed the activity itself. Although the former college football star loved the sensations of oral sex, however, he always grew uncomfortable after just a few moments, fearing that Sharon was getting bored and that he was being selfish. As a result, he usually rushed them to intercourse before she was really aroused. Not surprisingly, she didn't enjoy it that much and noticed she was starting to find excuses for avoiding sex altogether.

During our second session, I asked the pleasant middle-aged couple to eliminate intercourse for sixty days. That meant that oral sex couldn't be "foreplay" anymore, which meant that there was no reason for John to rush through it. I also challenged John to trust Sharon's claim that she enjoyed fellatio, even though doing so was uncomfortable for him.

After several weeks, John reported that he was relaxing and enjoying fellatio quite a bit more. By our seventh session, Sharon said, "We haven't forgotten about intercourse, but we are having really good sex without it." When they resumed intercourse after two months, they kept the oral sex—not as something preparatory to intercourse, but as an activity to be enjoyed for itself. Once they were getting lost in various kinds of stimulation, they had intercourse only when they were excited. As a result, Sharon reports, "Intercourse is the best it's ever been—when we remember to have it!"

Your Erotic Vision

People are used to thinking of sex as "going somewhere," and they're used to evaluating what they're doing at a given moment in light of where the sex is "going." So it's understandable that the idea of "There's nowhere to go; you're already there" may make you nervous. It takes away the grounding people rely upon, which allows them to avoid being completely immersed in the sexual experience. The idea really does acknowledge the subjectivity of sexuality in a clear, radical way. And while many people give this idea lip service, few really take it seriously.

Interestingly, this change in our relationship to what we do sexually (i.e., adding a level of infinite possibility) also changes our relationship to the outside world—adding a level of infinite possibility. Once all of you is an erotic being, and all erotic activities are equal, the entire world is a sex toy. An elevator becomes a place to rub up against your mate and get him excited. A scarf becomes something to tease your partner's neck with. Those dance shows on TV? You can turn down the sound and watch the people gyrate, supplying your own story line. You and your partner can walk down the street and speculate about the kind of underwear the other pedestrians are wearing—if any.

When you discard intercourse as the primary way to understand sex, eroticism in its various aspects itself becomes the central theme of sexuality. And when not limited to seeing it in the context of intercourse, we can see it everywhere, in everything. *There is almost nothing that is inherently non-erotic;* we make things erotic or not by the way we relate to them. For example, wearing a blindfold can be sexy, boring, aggravating, or scary. Having your nipples pinched can be sexy, neutral, or annoying. Each of these can feel consensual or hostile.

Of course, some things require more imagination to be seen as sexy than others, but that's about us, not the things themselves. A nurse's outfit can be scary or sexy, as can a nun's habit, military uniform, parochial school skirt, airplane bathroom, facial hair, and being held down during sex. Only a century ago, what we now scorn as "pasty white skin" was adored as "alabaster," "milky," "pure," and "snowy."

So let's explore this alternative erotic vision, in which almost anything can be erotic and the world is a sex toy. Using the outercourse paradigm discussed in Part II (in contrast to the intercourse paradigm discussed in chapters 1 through 4), we'll examine what sex can actually be like. Note that we won't say much about what to do with your body parts; outercourse is more about changing your mind than arranging your body.

Notice how much becomes possible once you change paradigms. Here's what's actually involved.

PRESENCE (VS. "PERFORMANCE")

The number-one facilitator of sexual satisfaction isn't performance, a perfect body (another kind of performance), or romantic love. It's presence: being all there when you're there.

In our pragmatic, action-oriented culture, something as intangible as presence doesn't get talked about much. But most of us can tell if our partner isn't all there during sex, and we usually know when we aren't. Reflect on your own sexual experiences, and you'll see how much the quality of presence contributes to your satisfaction, and how much its lack detracts from it.

CASE

Ann and Her New Boyfriend

With previous sexual partners, Ann has always let herself moan and writhe when she felt good. This usually added to the cosmetic saleswoman's excitement, and this positive spiral typically culminated in a big orgasm. With her new boyfriend, however, Ann was feeling self-conscious during sex for the first time.

After a few sessions, she realized it was because she doesn't feel that he's totally into their sex together; "I guess I feel like he's always holding back some little part of himself," the stylish ex–New Yorker said, shaking her head. "It makes it hard for me to trust him and to completely let go myself." Watching herself become inhibited because of her boyfriend's incomplete presence disturbed Ann greatly. She tried to discuss it with him, but he was always defensive, refusing to take her upset seriously. It was one of the main reasons they eventually broke up: "*My* being present during sex is really important to me," she said one afternoon. "I don't want anything in my life that undermines that."

The extent to which you're present during sex depends on you and you alone. This means that if you take responsibility for your own degree of presence, you gain control over a large aspect of your sexual encounters.

At the same time, the nature of presence means that you can't fake it for very long, and that difficult emotions interrupt it. There's simply no substitute for it: big breasts, more thrusting, or louder moaning can't compensate for someone's incomplete presence. It's similar to the way no amount of salt can make up for food being undercooked. That's part of what people mean when they talk about being vulnerable during sex. Your self is out there on display, and your partner typically knows if there isn't enough of your self there.

For people used to focusing a great deal on performance, the very issue of presence is disconcerting. It seems to involve paying attention to the wrong thing—to *being* rather than to *doing*. And it requires trusting that things that had previously been important (such as erection and physical beauty) will take care of themselves. It also requires trust in your own body and in the value of eroticism. This can be complicated, because we've been systematically taught *not* to trust our sexuality, and to consider it dirty, undependable, irrelevant, or unknowable.

What are the qualities of "being there"? How can you improve the degree of your presence during sexual encounters?

- You feel your body: you're focused on physical sensation much more than you're thinking about anything.
- You use your senses to connect to your partner: you look, you smell, and you taste, involving your partner in your experience.
- You don't distract yourself: if unplanned or unwanted things happen, you either take advantage of them or you let them go as quickly as possible.
- You take responsibility for your own presence: if you're not as present as you'd like to be, you do things to change that: talk to your partner, check on whatever you're thinking about, write a reminder to yourself, etc.
- You enjoy what you're doing: or you find a way to enjoy it, or

you switch to a different erotic activity. Or you decide that you don't want to be sexual right now—which is also a form of presence, as you maintain your awareness of yourself and align what you're doing with what you want.

SPIRITUALITY AND TRANCE

Here's a definition of spirituality that you may find useful:

- an awareness that the universe contains *something* bigger than us; and
- an awareness that that *something* is not completely knowable by rational means; and
- a sense of connection with that *something*.

Yearly polls, and the popularity of religion, New Age programs, and Eastern teachings, make it clear that Americans desire and value a spiritual dimension to life. In fact, the more our families and communities splinter, the more most people yearn to feel connected to something divine, sacred, or metaphysical.

Sexuality can be a splendid vehicle for spirituality—a way of experiencing it, coming closer to it, being more comfortable with it. This is true, however, only to the extent that you are able to pay attention to this alternative reality, and not be completely caught up in unwanted thoughts or feelings. When intercourse is the center of our sexual expression, we tend to focus on *performance*—a rational, *nonspiritual* thing. So to facilitate the spiritual side of sexual experience, it's important to deemphasize intercourse, especially its performance aspect.

"Trance" describes the state of surrendering to nonrational experience. Trance is the pathway to spirituality in sex. That is, sex is a gentle way temporarily to leave the mundane world—its pressures, its cares, its conflicts, its disappointments. This experience can be even more rewarding than the pleasure or orgasm you get from sex. While you may not always choose to use sex like that, the option is *always there.*

Being in a sexual trance with a partner is lovely. It involves losing track of your body a bit; forgetting about time, or even where you are; a heightening of one or more senses (the gentlest touch may feel profound, the simplest tones may sound beautiful); seeing the metaphysical dimension of your connection; and temporarily letting go of your mental pictures about how the world is, surrendering to a mutual *something* with your partner, creating a special bond. In this state you've both left the world of logical reasoning, so there's nothing *out there* with which to evaluate your sex—all you have is the experience. While in a trance, partners often feel they can actually sense each other's experience. You and your partner feel that you're in a very special place together.

The nice thing about being in a sexual trance is how our bodies function in this state. When you're in a trance, you let your body follow its own wisdom, without trying to use your conscious mind to control it. Thus, reflex and intuition run the show. That's when your body functions perfectly well, regardless of how you might otherwise judge it. In this state, for example, a man might enjoy exquisite sensations on his penis—and not get erect. A kiss might feel like an absolutely complete erotic experience, in which you might get lost for so long that you have no need to do anything else.

But you can only approach a trance state when you're *not* focused on the various imperatives of intercourse, such as timing and performance. These linear, somewhat nerve-racking issues can keep you anchored in anxiety and negative fantasies, rather than allowing you to focus on the perfection of your body and your sexuality right here, right now. So one more reason to deempha size intercourse is to get more access to sexuality's spiritual dimension.

Since what you want from sex probably involves connection, intimacy, and emotional relaxation as well as physical pleasure, try consciously experimenting with making sex more spiritual. This is *not* because sexuality needs to be justified by a spiritual dimension. Rather, it can be a great way for you to get more of what you want from sex.

Many people think the primary or only way to enhance the intimacy of sex is through romantic love. Although this works for some people, for most it isn't sufficient, and for others it's unnecessary. Because we westerners don't live in a spiritually oriented or sex-positive culture, most of us don't think of sex as a spiritual practice. Antisex religious beliefs complicate the matter. But if you wish, here are some tools that will enhance the spirituality of your sexual expression—which can enhance the nonsexual part of your life as well. By the way, note how the following are similar to the suggestions you just read for enhancing your sexual "presence."

- Before sex, prepare by quieting your mind. Various people do this with meditation, a few minutes of stretching, a hot bath, or focusing on special music.
- Breathe deeply during sex. This will help your body relax, quiet the chatter in your mind, and let you realize how extraordinary the capacity to be sexual really is.
- Maintain eye contact with your partner during sex. This will

help you connect with your partner, while excluding most other things from your consciousness.

- Experience your body's perfection during sex. Notice how good kissing doesn't require you to lose weight; notice how having more hair or whiter teeth wouldn't make your orgasms any better. In this sense, sex can be a mental vacation from all the self-criticism your body endures. Also, notice how, if you suspend your thoughts, your body's wisdom finds ways of feeling connected to your partner's body. In this sense, your body *wants* to be spiritual.
- Don't judge anything that happens during sex. If this is too difficult, select a single minute, any minute, and don't judge anything during that time. This can be another wonderful mental vacation. As you strip away the layers of self-criticism and society's expectations, you will find yourself naturally drifting closer to the world of nature and spirit—and relaxation.

Notice that none of these ideas is specifically about intercourse—there's no mention of penis or vagina, erection, lubrication, thrusting, or orgasm. The focus here is on a different dimension of sex altogether. This isn't to say that intercourse can't be spiritual; but if it is, it's spiritual not because it's intercourse but regardless of the fact that it's intercourse.

WHY BREATHING IS SEX/SEXUAL/SEXY

We do it thousands of times each day with no thought whatsoever—breathing. And yet breathing is one of the sexiest things you can do.

For one thing, you do it in your body, where sex occurs.

Breathing is a lovely way for people to connect. When you and your partner lie quietly together and match your breathing, it creates instant intimacy, as well as a readiness to connect your bodies more deeply. Breathing shallowly—as when you're anxious or resentful—inhibits sexual feelings. Breathing deeply encourages these feelings. By encouraging oxygen and blood flow, it also encourages vasodilation and other sexual reflexes. When you get aroused, breathing facilitates the flow of erotic energy in your body. And breathing can actually affect emotions—breathing shallowly reinforces anxiety, while breathing deeply creates relaxation.

So breathing is a technology. Don't underestimate it just because it's so simple. After all, some of the simplest technologies changed the world—such as the wheel and making fire.

Some cultures take breathing so seriously that people spend decades mastering it. These Eastern and traditional cultures know that breathing is a way of shaping sexual experience, something that many of us want to do but don't know how. So don't disdain it. And if focusing on your breathing to enhance your erotic experience sounds like too much effort, what are you saying about the value of your sexuality?

SENSUALITY

Sensuality simply involves the stimulation and gratification of the physical senses. In a sexual context, the point is to open and expand your consciousness of these physical senses—to wake up and delight yourself (and your partner). Since nothing can be considered "foreplay" without intercourse, these sensual activities aren't supposed to take you somewhere—they are for enjoyment *right now*. And yet, as you enjoy them, you will often look forward to eroticism, whether now or at some unspecified time later.

Sensual activities can open and arouse you *before* genital play, making the subsequent eroticism more intense and personal. So spend some time and explore both old and new pleasure zones, including (but not limited to) the nipples, ears, neck, anus, back, mouth, and hairline. In no particular order, here's a *very* partial list of sensual activities you can do with your partner.

Shower or bathe together: not to get clean, but for the fun of it. Light the bathroom with candles. Then use plenty of soap, splash around, and slowly wash your partner's hair (remember, the shampoo bottles always say lather, rinse, *repeat*). Dry each other, not yourselves.

Music: Don't settle for the radio; every great movie has a soundtrack, and here's the chance to program yours. Play a tape or CD you like, loud enough to hear, but not loud enough to interfere with conversation. And don't limit yourself to "romantic" or "background" music. Play something you enjoy.

Textures: Assemble a group of "touch toys," including smooth stones, pieces of satin and silk, a feather or two, and some leather. Touch your partner with them while you both slow down and focus your attention on this one sense. Take a few objects and handle them, eyes closed, without figuring out what they are.

Flowers: Flowers are designed by nature to attract the attention of simple creatures. Spend $5 for a week's worth of stimulation, and take advantage of the chance to focus on something without thinking.

Kissing: Slow, teasing, with and without nibbling. Experiment with different flavors (candy, fruit) and temperatures (ice, hot tea). And kiss beyond your partner's mouth: Kiss his/her face, eyes, neck. Kiss the rest of your partner's body, and don't forget the ice and hot tea while you do.

Food and drink: Put a few simple things on the night table—fruit, crackers, juice—and decide to taste them as if you've never had them before. Not only will you enjoy this, your newly awakened mouth will also find kissing and licking a revelation. Even a simple glass of water by the bed will enable you to honor your thirst during sex instead of ignoring it.

Whisper: It almost doesn't matter what you say when you whisper. Voices sound different; you have to get closer to each other; you wind up stimulating each other's delicate ear tissue; and you effectively block out the rest of world. If you're embarrassed to say how you feel or what you want, describe what you'd say if you weren't embarrassed.

Lubricants: There are now dozens of sexual lubricants available at sex shops, in supermarkets and drugstores, and through the mail. Don't use them because you need to; use them because they're fun, they increase pleasure, and they're a great excuse to touch each other. When you get into bed, take your lube out and put it right out there with your water, tissues, snacks, and other erotic supplies.

Masturbation: Here's your chance to show your mate what you like and how you like it. It is so sexy to watch someone pleasure him/herself, losing him/herself in the feelings, remembering his/her body is perfect. And it is so sexy to be watched by someone who thinks you're desireable to start with (he/she's already in bed with you, right?). Touch yourself as if for the first time, discovering what feels good. Make your usual noises, and hear what they sound like. Eyes open or closed? Your call.

HEALING WOUNDS FROM AN INTERCOURSE-ORIENTED WORLD

A lot of what is called sexual dysfunction is the result of narrow, intercourse-focused thinking. As you saw in Part I, it isn't just the limitations of individuals' thinking; it's a society-wide problem—people wounded by living in an intercourse-oriented world. As shown by the stories throughout this book (and perhaps your own experience as well), those wounds are expressed as problems of desire, orgasm, erection, and sexual guilt, boredom, self-loathing, anxiety, shame, and inhibition.

These wounds are as serious as any other psychological wounds, affecting people for their entire lives. These wounds can even influence people's childrearing (attitudes about sex education, punishing masturbation or childhood sexplay, etc.), thus making these wounds intergenerational, like other forms of sexualized trauma. Our culture should take these wounds more seriously, through better training for physicians, psychologists, and other clinicians working with sexual issues. America also needs the mass media to relate less to improving people's "normal" sexuality and more to enhancing their comfort with their own eroticism.

Reducing your focus on intercourse is a key element in healing those wounds. It's the first step toward reclaiming your erotic rights—your body, feelings, internal experience. Once you've done this, you can decide for yourself what sexual agendas, choices, and behaviors you want—based on your needs, not on your desire to conform to a model.

CASE

Is Jennifer "Frigid"?

Jennifer was a college student who was attractive and popular. Although she dated a lot in high school, the accounting student had remained a virgin. "Well, pretty much a virgin," she said quietly. "Some playing around, but that's all." Several of her boyfriends had urged her to make love with them, but she had always refused. She loved to kiss, and she always enjoyed plenty of that from her dates. She enjoyed sensual touching, too, especially caressing and being caressed under her clothes, and there was no shortage of that either.

Once at college the pressure to have intercourse intensified. When a sophomore she really liked encouraged her to have "real sex," she relented. "The sex was okay," she said, idly twirling a strand of her dark brown hair, "but suddenly the other stuff practically disappeared. There was less kissing, less cuddling and giggling together, it was just different all of a sudden. It was really disappointing."

Her loss was ironic, since those relational sorts of things were mostly what she wanted from being sexual. She had been perfectly content to masturbate her boyfriends whenever they wanted—they were always so appreciative, and afterward they'd cuddle and laugh and say they loved her. As many young people discover, however, once she started having intercourse with someone, it was extremely hard to turn back the clock—and at that age, almost no one has the communication skills to create an alternative scenario.

Only recently, in fact, Jennifer had become so frustrated about sex that she abruptly stopped having intercourse, at which point her boyfriend left her. Now she had neither sex nor touching, and she thought the problem was her. "I guess I'm frigid or something," she softly cried. "I'll never be able to have a good relationship." As her therapist, my goal was helping her get past the question of whether or not she was "frigid" (a completely unhelpful, obsolete clinical term), to helping her see her situation as a more complicated male-female dynamic. But it was important that she understand that her preference for non-intercourse eroticism was certainly *not* the problem.

CASE

Mae's Secret

Mae was extremely passionate and enjoyed sex a great deal—as long as it involved plenty of oral stimulation. "To me, that's the most intimate kind of sex," the Hong Kong native said during her first session. "When a man goes down on me and seems to enjoy it, I feel like he accepts me in an important way.

"But a lot of men think of cunnilingus as just foreplay, and then I feel rushed," she explained. "And if they think it's just to get me hot, while I think it's the main event, I feel a little like a freak. So it's like my secret. I pretend it's just foreplay, but I'm thinking, If I can get him to do it long enough, I'll come, and then I'll go along with the intercourse kind of like dessert. And he can have a great time if he wants. But I feel dishonest, because I have sort of a plan that I'm hiding.

"So for a long time I had a double problem," the short, perfectly groomed realtor said. "Like a lot of women, I thought I was ugly down there, which was terrible because I always wanted my sexual partners to spend a lot of time down there. But I also thought there was something wrong with my vagina because I wasn't so thrilled with, you know, real sex. It was weird—I knew I liked sex; I just didn't like regular sex. In fact, I even got so worried about myself one summer that I tried giving up sex altogether. But that definitely didn't work." She half-smiled, shaking her head.

"I still wonder if my vagina is totally normal, although at least I know my clitoris works real well. But I still have this secret going on, which always makes sex less relaxed than it probably should be. God, I wish sex were simpler."

Other people manifest their intercourse-based wounds in other ways. Some men feel tremendous performance pressure, which they unconsciously express through erection problems. When their partners respond with anger or criticism, they exacerbate the guilt and shame these men already feel, causing even more relationship problems.

Many women who have perfectly good orgasms don't climax from intercourse. When their partners feel inadequate or anxious, they sometimes respond by attacking or attempting to mentor the women, which can also destroy a relationship. Without question, many relationships are unnecessarily undermined or destroyed when partners challenge each other's adequacy or question their own, all because someone's sexual expression doesn't fit the intercourse-centered model. There are few things more painful than to have your partner look at you and say, "The way you function sexually proves you don't love or desire me"—especially when you know your body functions just fine in its preferred sexual contexts.

COMMUNICATION

Outercourse is custom-designed sex. Since you and your partner both start practically from scratch each time, without performance standards and ideas of "foreplay" to guide you, you have to talk while you build. Otherwise, you can find yourselves in a sexual Tower of Babel—wanting to cooperate but, without a language, simply unable to do so. It's as if you and your partner were working on an assembly line together, but one of you is building a sports car and the other a jeep—and you've become resentful toward each other for doing the "wrong thing."

Since outercourse typically demands more communication from participants, it can be a vehicle around which people can bond emotionally. The communication that you develop to facilitate outercourse lingers after the sex is over, and sweetens the entire relationship. It's like the flowers you take home from someone's wedding, which you enjoy after the actual event is over.

In the next chapter we'll answer some common communication questions that people have about sex.

THE INTERCOURSE SABBATICAL

As you have already seen, most sex therapists prescribe a ban on intercourse (not sex, just intercourse) as part of treating a number of different sexual problems. The very reasons this is helpful for solving problems also make it valuable for people *without* problems.

An intercourse sabbatical is simply a mutual decision not to have intercourse for a defined period, regardless of how much one or the other partner might desire it during this time. This greatly reduces the pressure to get an erection, removes the necessity for contraception, and virtually eliminates vaginal lubrication as an issue.

The temporary agreement does even more: it forces you to construct a satisfying sex life from whatever is left over—which is anything you're willing to try. And you can try pretty much anything you and your partner want to. Since there's no more "foreplay" while you're doing this, you never know exactly where you are in a sexual encounter, and you get to learn to tolerate that. That's a lot of opportunity, all from one little sabbatical.

How long should your intercourse sabbatical be? There is no "right" length for this experiment. It does have to be long enough for you to be sexual together a number of times. For some people, that will be a few weeks; others might require many months to create the desired effect.

Sex therapists find that about a quarter of the patients who agree to this as an assignment "slip" and have intercourse during the sabbatical. For couples who haven't had any sex in years (many of whom get this assignment too, remember), this "mistake" is often positive, the beginning of a successful if arduous journey back to periodic lovemaking. For other couples it can be an expression of passion, carelessness, anxiety about sexual intimacy, or hostility toward the therapy. If you "slip" while trying this sabbatical, don't worry. Talking with your partner about how it happened, how each of you made your decision, and what you've learned about yourselves, each other, and sex can be extremely valuable, not to mention very intimate.

As you construct your sabbatical, remember that this isn't supposed to be a deprivation, but rather an opportunity (even if it's occasionally uncomfortable). Above all, *do not impose this* on your partner. Approach him or her with the idea, discuss the benefits and disadvantages, and come to a decision together. Any other approach invites resentment and resistance.

VARIATIONS ON THE INTERCOURSE SABBATICAL

The intercourse sabbatical is designed to help you make an erotic breakthrough. By reducing performance pressure and getting you out of old habits, it enables you to experiment with new sexual perspectives and behaviors.

But it's possible to get this result without abstaining from intercourse completely. So if you like, give one or more of these sabbatical variations a try. Whichever you choose, the point is to find new ways to explore and express your eroticism.

Therefore, for a period of time you and your partner select together (no less than eight weeks), have intercourse *only* . . .

. . . after a mutual, *self-revealing conversation*.

Talk about yourself, not about your mate.

. . . after the person initiating has said something *self-revealing* and new.

Again, talk about yourself—a feeling, preference, or experience that your mate doesn't know about you.

. . . after a discussion of any *non*sexual reasons the two of you prefer intercourse right now.

For example, "full-body contact would be great right now." Be specific about it: "I like smelling your hair," "The pressure of your body on mine makes me feel taken care of," etc. You can then proceed to intercourse or not, as you choose.

. . . after the woman has had an *orgasm* by other means.

But use this only if she won't feel pressured by it.

. . . after the man's erection is allowed to *subside,* and he then regains it.

But use this only if partners agree to be good-natured if he doesn't get the erection back.

. . . when both people are wide *awake.*

It might be helpful to set an arbitrary time (say, 10 P.M.) after which you won't initiate sex. Many couples notice that if they don't make love right before going to sleep, it's harder to initiate sex because it's more explicit. Talk with your mate about this.

. . . after some *sensuous activity,* such as listening to music, feeding each other with fingers, or bathing together.

Enjoy the sensuality itself; you'll either get to intercourse or you won't.

. . . for a *specified amount of time* (say, two minutes), and then stop.

At that point continue with other erotic activities. You can alternate intercourse and outercourse several times. Will one of you lead, or will you do this together?

. . . when partner A *initiates* during the first four-week block. Then have intercourse only when partner B initiates during the second four-week block. Do this for a cycle of sixteen weeks, then evaluate. What did you like about this? Dislike?

COMBINING INTERCOURSE AND OUTERCOURSE

So you're interested in all this outercourse stuff. Now you have information, encouragement, and a new vision of sexuality. Where do you go from here?

Anywhere you want. Actually, the next step is combining intercourse and outercourse. And with your new perspective, that should be an exciting challenge; by now, you have tools to make both intercourse and outercourse different. The best outcome is seeing intercourse in the wholesome, pressure-free environment that outercourse can help you create.

When it's not the centerpiece of your sex life, intercourse has the potential to be more interesting. In general, because you can be less anxious to complete it and do it "right" and less concerned about protecting yourself, it's easier to have fun and to create the emotional connection and other experiences that you want. And, as we've seen, you may be less "dysfunctional" as a result, if that's been a problem.

As with outercourse, the trick is to see intercourse as a set of opportunities, rather than a task to complete correctly. With this attitude, you can experiment—you can stop and start, change rhythms, laugh, discover new positions, talk with your partner and generate even more ideas. When you're not worried about doing sex "normally" or the "right way," everything your partner says is simply information, and you can't make mistakes.

Many people talk about wanting more variety within long-term sexual relationships. Your new outercourse perspective adds a lovely unpredictability to *all* sex, including intercourse. Now, any single sexual moment has its own integrity, and you can get so far into it that you don't know—and don't care—what's next.

CASE

Mark and Rita's Sabbatical

Why did Mark and Rita come to see me? "Simple," the tall, slim security guard told me. "Boredom. Rita and I love each other, but sex has become routine, boring, unexciting. When she joked a few weeks ago that maybe we should each have an affair, I knew we needed help. Fast."

After getting to know them a little, I believed that they did, in fact, love each other. They also *liked* each other, which is important in long-term relationships. After all, love can only get you so far.

But they were very disappointed with how their lovemaking had dwindled in frequency, excitement, and importance. We talked at length about the impact this had on the rest of their relationship and dealt with the anger, sadness, and self-criticism they each felt. They then agreed to an eight-week ban on intercourse. During that time, they did weekly home assignments involving various kinds of sensual touch and pleasure. Gradually, their interest in sex with each other increased. Soon they were having and enjoying non-intercourse sex every Saturday, and occasionally more often than that.

When the eight weeks eventually expired, it was time to reintroduce intercourse. "What," I asked them, "have you learned about outercourse that you particularly like?" "Deemphasizing orgasm," said Rita. "Being more spontaneous, doing whatever we like in any order," said Mark. "Oh, and checking in with each other during sex," added Rita. "I really like knowing where Mark's head is when we're having sex, and now we do that pretty easily."

So this is where we started. "Well, how are you going to make those features part of intercourse, as well as outercourse?" I challenged them. Together, we came up with a long list of suggestions, some of which you may find helpful:

—During the week, visualize the kind of spontaneous, playful, intimate sex you'd like, rather than imagining the sex you don't want.

—Practice deep breathing thirty seconds a day. Be aware of your body—temperature, moisture, muscle tension—and bring this awareness into your lovemaking. Deep breathing facilitates deep arousal.

—Maintain eye contact during sex, and periodically ask yourself if you know how your partner feels right now. If you don't think you know, pay more attention, or ask (or both).

—During sex, focus on the present. Anytime you think of the future or the past, refocus on the present, whether it's how something feels in your body, or some feature of your partner's body you particularly enjoy.

—During sex, ask yourself several times: Is this what I want to do or feel right now? If it isn't, change what you're doing.

"WE WANT A BABY; HOW CAN WE DEEMPHASIZE INTERCOURSE?"

Couples who work too hard at conceiving can damage their sex life and entire relationship. Ironically, they sometimes don't conceive, either. Well-meaning friends and family tell such couples to "relax";

indeed, there is a physiological basis to this advice. Besides, anxiety and resentment are no foundation from which to launch a new life.

We believe that if you enjoy other kinds of sexual activity during the time you're attempting to conceive, you'll feel closer to your partner, your bodies will function better (erection and lubrication), and intercourse will be easier.

CASE

The Baby-Making Dentists

Mario and Lise were dentists in their late thirties when they married. Now they had everything they wanted, including frequent, exciting sex. All that was missing was a baby, which these high-powered problem-solvers figured was no sweat. What they hadn't counted on was a slight fertility abnormality, and the effect that their goal-directed, no-nonsense approach to conception would have on the rest of their lives.

They tried to do everything perfectly, going about the desired conception with extreme efficiency. They wrote up a schedule detailing when they should have intercourse. They forgot only one small thing: This was supposed to be lovemaking! "Sex has sure stopped being fun," Mario said glumly three months after they started the routine.

They valued sex a great deal and now were, in a sense, mourning the loss of a key part of their recreational and intimate life. So I encouraged them to take a small "procreation sabbatical" at least once during each fertile period, having outercourse and "wasting" an opportunity to conceive each month. This, I reasoned, would help them feel more in charge of their lives, and help them remember what they had in mind when they decided to conceive. "I want you to have great, pointless sex," I challenged, "the way you used to. Without intercourse. Just pleasure, closeness, abandon."

And it worked. They once again had the kind of sex that kept them each personally centered, grounded in the relationship they treasured. Suddenly, the baby-making project wasn't running away with their marriage anymore. "When we find ourselves trying too hard, we remember the great sex we had just a day or two ago, and it really relaxes us," said Lise. "It's a lot easier now to just say 'It'll happen when it happens.' "

They conceived three months after they resumed enjoying sex.

Chapter 8

Communication Q & A

As we have discussed, satisfying outercourse requires communication. But most of us are specifically taught *not* to talk about sex seriously or honestly. We're told things like "That isn't for mixed company" or "It isn't ladylike to say that" or "Talking about sex isn't romantic" or "It takes the mystery away." Even today, many school sex education programs do not include the accurate names for body parts, and they often separate girls from boys—even though each needs to learn how to talk to the other. And we *never* see TV or film characters talk honestly with each other about sex—from *Beverly Hills 90210* to *As Good As It Gets,* people are sexual without ever discussing what they like or don't like, and they *never discuss* birth control or health issues. So it would be surprising if people did *not* run into communication difficulties around sexuality. This chapter answers some common questions people have about sexual communication.

"All the words involving sex sound dirty or medical. What should I do?"

Words, of course, are the basis of communication. But as George Bernard Shaw said, "We don't think of sex decently, so we have no decent words for sex." We have street language, slang, and the language of our private thoughts, and then way over there, only vaguely related to real life, we have medical language, most of which is based on Latin. Somehow, "fellatio" doesn't sound like what it feels like, and "vulva" doesn't sound like what it looks like.

But "down there," "y'know," and "the regular way" just aren't good enough. They aren't clear. They don't really foster a sense of relaxation, mastery, or closeness. And as we've seen, outercourse demands more communication than intercourse, not less. We're stuck: we need words.

So choose some words, any words, and make them your own. Try some Latin—with a wink, a caress, or a giggle. Or try some slang—with a salute, funny face, or eyes covered. Once you do, these words won't sound any more peculiar than "herring," "scud missile," "patent leather," or "luge."

"Can't we be spontaneous? Why do we need all this sexual communication?"

Long ago, sex could be more or less spontaneous. But now, every day is loaded with sexual stimulation: sexy freeway billboards, music on the car radio, stylish clothes, magazine covers, jokes around the office water cooler, TV shows. Sex in America will *never* be truly spontaneous again.

If all you want is a quick orgasm or possibly creating a pregnancy, sex can be done somewhat spontaneously, without much communication. But most of us have much higher expectations of sex: we want it to be intimate, validating, comfortable, authentic, and fun, in addition to orgasmic. Perhaps you want sex to be spiritual, comforting, or a way of sharing or expressing love. For this more sophisticated outcome, we need to communicate. A *lot*. It's like the difference between building a hut and building a mansion. The latter job would require that the crew communicate a *lot* more.

Sex can include plenty of spontaneity if you *plan* a little. This may sound paradoxical, but consider a picnic. Let's say we agree we'll go next Saturday. We decide that one of us will buy sandwiches and drinks, while the other brings a radio, Frisbee, and blanket. We get a map to the place, fill the car with gas, and bring sunscreen. There's lots of planning—but once we get there, it all pays off. We can do whatever we like, in any order: eat before playing Frisbee, play Frisbee first, or skip Frisbee altogether. The planning makes the spontaneity possible. Of course, if all you want from a "picnic" is being in a grassy park for an hour, you can do so without much preparation, and feel pretty free. But if you decide you want to eat, listen to music, play Frisbee, or avoid a sunburn, you'll wish you had done some planning.

Sex is like that. You prepare: you get your contraception (if necessary), pour a glass of water and put in on the night table, use the bathroom, lock the bedroom door if you have kids, etc. And you have a communication system: words you both understand, agreements on how to talk with each other, special ways of touching. Then you can do whatever you like, in any order, even make up new things you've never done, not knowing how they'll turn out—*now* you can be as spontaneous as you like. Love that planning, love that communication system. Together, they make everything possible in bed.

Here's a sample conversation:

A: Why do we have to communicate about everything? I want sex to be spontaneous.

B: I know. It's fun to just jump into it without a lot of fuss.

A: Yeah, but you stop me and run off to the bathroom, or you want to have a conversation, or whatever. You interrupt the mood. And I think you keep yourself from getting excited that way.

B: Well, maybe there are ways I can do things that don't get in your way so much. Still, I like communicating, and I like preparing so sex is more the way I enjoy it.

A: Yeah, but I remember when I was young we didn't worry about all this communicating. We just did it and it was great.

B: (laughing): Oh, no problems? No worries? Everything just the way you wanted it?

A: Well, not exactly . . .

B: Right. We didn't know any better back then. Now we can make choices. A little preparation goes a long way. And we can make it sexy instead of a hassle. You know, like tasting while you cook makes you more excited about what you're going to serve later. Or the way you prepare to watch a big game on TV: by collecting your chips and beer, reading the team rosters, fluffing your pillow, and closing the blinds behind the TV. It's part of getting psyched up for the game, right?

A: Right. I get ready for the game. But that's different.

B: Well, maybe not so different. Besides, when your brother Bill comes over to watch with you, he doesn't understand about you getting ready for the game, and it bugs you.

A: Yeah, how could he enjoy it without knowing what's going on, and then getting up in the middle of the exciting part to get the beer he's brought over—which half the time he hasn't even put on ice? Where is his head?

B: I guess he's enjoying the game at a different level than you.

A: Definitely.

B: Right—just like sex. We can choose what level we want to enjoy it on.

A: Ah ha . . .

B: Honey, I want the more sophisticated kind of sex, the kind that requires some planning and communication. And it's not because I want to create distance—just the opposite. I want to feel close to you when we make love, and for that I need preparation and communication. When you talk with me and listen to me during sex, it's much easier to create a good time.

A: Well, I do want that.

B: Well, that's what it takes.

A: I see. *Hmm* [or some other thoughtful sound] that puts it in a different light.

"This may sound dumb, but can you give me examples of how to ask for what I want?"

Many people get stuck on the language of "asking," so you might find it helpful to rehearse different styles of voicing your desires and preferences. These include:

May I . . . ?

Will you . . . ?

I would love it if . . .

I think I would like to try . . .

How would you feel about . . . ?

You wouldn't want to . . . , would you?

Hey, what do you say we . . . ?

You know, I've been dreaming of . . .

It would mean so much to me if we . . .

It sure sounded good when I heard about . . .

I really need . . .

I want you to . . .

Please don't . . .

It doesn't feel comfortable for me when . . .

You must never . . .

I'm begging you to . . .

Please, will you . . .

I think it's important for our relationship that we . . .

Brainstorming outside of the situation helps loosen up your ability to know what you want and to talk about it, and it helps reduce anxiety and embarrassment. It's helpful to imagine being *in*appropriate, too; after you visualize demanding, threatening, manipulating, bullying, whining, and begging, simply stating what you want seems pretty innocuous.

"My partner doesn't want to cooperate in exploring new things."

Here's a conversation you might have:

A: So I've been reading this book about sex, and it's pretty interesting.

B: Some book about how all men are dogs? Great.

A: No, you're not that bad (smiles). No, this is a book about getting beyond intercourse.

B: To what—talking about feelings? Watching football on TV?

A: Wow, you seem uncomfortable about this. I'd like us both to feel close and warm—is there a way you'd rather I talk about this?

B: Okay, okay, what's the deal with the book?

A: It's about a different style of sex. Instead of focusing on doing what we think is "normal," we tune in to what we really want and feel, and then kind of make up the sex to suit our personal desires.

B: So if I desire a few more people in our bed . . .

A: Well, we can discuss anything, although inviting a crowd into our bed is not something I'm into. But seriously, the point is to focus less on intercourse and more on other stuff.

B: Whoa, wait. It's taken us a while to finally get the intercourse thing down. At least that's predictable and it works. Why mess that up?

A: No, the object isn't to mess that up. It's just that sometimes people, well, get into a rut. C'mon, be honest with me: surely I'm not the only one around here who feels like that.

B: No.

A: Right, so maybe one of the reasons we're in a rut is we figure that when we have sex, sooner or later we'll have intercourse as usual, and everything else is just foreplay.

B: And the alternative is to just give up sex?

A: You mean give up intercourse? No, that's not the point. The idea is to experiment and talk to each other about what we enjoy and just kind of wander into stuff we both like and do whatever we want.

B: A couple would have to be pretty friendly to do that.

A: Right.

B: And probably have to trust each other—like if something didn't work, the other person wouldn't criticize you, or if you said what you liked, the other person wouldn't make fun of you.

A: Right.

B: You think we're there?

A: To be honest, not as much as we could be. But I think we could get there. This conversation is a good start.

B: So you want to try this new stuff?

A: Well, I'd like to talk about it a little, and yes, I'd like to try at least a different attitude. We might not even do such different stuff, but maybe with a different attitude, the sex would *feel* different. And I think we'd both like that.

B: Yeah, I agree.

A: So what I'd like is, um, that when we talk about this you don't make fun of me, and you don't accuse me of trying to control our sex life.

B: Okay.

A: And I'd like you to ask more questions about what I like or how I feel during sex. That way we can be more like a team. And I'll do the same, so I can learn to please you better.

B: Well, I'm sure up for that.

A: Good, well, thanks for talking about this with me. C'mere and give me a kiss.

B: Ah, ready to go fool around?

A: Not right now—I have to help Bobby with his homework—but I'm sure closer to being in the mood now than I was an hour ago.

"My partner wants to do things I don't want to. How do I say no?"

Let's start with a not-so-successful conversation you might have had in the past:

A: So there's this outercourse thing I've heard about. It sounds okay. There's a lot of stuff we could do.

B: (wanting to be optimistic): Yes, more variety would be nice.

A: Y'know, there're so many things we've never done, or only tried a few times. This is our chance.

B: (getting nervous): Yeah . . . well . . . um, we don't have to do *everything*, right?

A: No, of course not. But there are some things we could try. Some new things. And then some old things. You know, if you're a little more open-minded this time . . .

B: (worst fears confirmed): . . . Wait, don't blame me. I'm open-minded, I just don't go for every single thing. There's nothing wrong with that.

A: (worst fears confirmed) See, there you go—uptight about sex, saying no to things before we even start. It's probably hopeless. We'll never do anything really interesting.

B: Well, no matter what we do, you'll never be satisfied. No wonder our sex life is a mess.

Let's try this again, differently. Let's say your mate has sexual desires you don't happen to share. Here are three things you can say to let him or her know that you're on the same team.

A (Your partner): So there's this outercourse thing I've heard about. It sounds okay. There's a lot of stuff we could do.

B (You): You know, there are things I don't want to try, at least not now. I know you're disappointed about that, and I'm sorry. But I'd rather focus on the things I'd like to do, maybe even think of some new things. Perhaps down the road we can come back to this other thing you're wanting now.

Or:

A (Your partner): So there's this outercourse thing I've heard about. It sounds okay. There's a lot of stuff we could do.

B: Listen, we don't have a problem here—I want to enjoy sex with you, and to experiment with new things. Let's not get so caught up in whether or not we do any one activity that we can't enjoy anything else.

Or:

A (Your partner): So there's this outercourse thing I've heard about. It sounds okay. There's a lot of stuff we could do.

B: For now, let's be sexual in the ways I feel most enthusiastic about. Not only will we both enjoy it, but we'll be reminded that we can be a good sexual partnership. Then let's build from there.

"I talk about my anxieties and my partner just laughs."

It really hurts to feel you're not being taken seriously, doesn't it? This needs to be discussed before you can accomplish anything else. So when you're not in the middle of being upset, tell your partner, and talk about yourself: I feel invisible, I feel diminished, I feel powerless, I feel distant from you, I don't know what to do to feel better, I hate not being able to trust you.

When you talk about yourself like this, no one can disagree with you. If someone tries (e.g., "You're such a baby," "You can't take a joke," "You're always uncomfortable about something"), don't defend yourself, which just invites more criticism. Instead, remind your partner of the one indisputable fact in the universe: how you feel. For example, "It may seem babyish to you, but this is how I feel, and I need us to take it seriously."

If your partner gets tired of this, point out that as soon as your feeling is accepted as valid for you, the two of you can move on to something more complex and action oriented: "I want to be comfortable experimenting with you sexually, but I can't do that until I feel safer and more visible. Will you be my teammate in changing how I feel?"

"When I ask for what I want, my partner freaks out. Is there a special way I should do it?"

Asking for what you want sexually can be an enormous contribution to a relationship (in addition to being the most effective way to get what you want). But that's assuming that you're genuinely asking for what you want, and not using a request to express hostility or to trap, embarrass, or manipulate someone. How do you ask? By asking. Do it when you're feeling close, and make plenty of eye contact. A hand on someone's shoulder or knee always helps to convey sincerity, and helps the other person feel connected to you.

Nonverbal communication can also be effective. Gently placing someone's hand where you want it, guiding it the way you like to be touched, and moving it when you don't like what's being done are all legitimate. Feel free to comment later on what you did, reinforcing the message and eliminating any possible misinterpretation. For example, you might want to say, "Remember when I moved your hand while we were making love yesterday? It's not that I mind when you squeeze my breasts—I like that—I just prefer you not pull my nipples while you do it."

Every sexual couple needs ways to ask for things without fear of the other person being offended. If you and your partner haven't worked this out, talk about it when you're *not* in bed. For example, you might say, "Carl, I'd like to feel comfortable asking for what I want when we make love. How would you like me to do that?" Remember, telling your partner what you want is a great gift. Don't you feel that way about your partner telling you his/her preferences? Don't hesitate to say so: "Maria, I really like when you let me know what pleases you. It helps me relax because I don't have to worry that you're secretly hoping for something else, or praying that something uncomfortable will end."

"My partner refuses to talk about sex, period. What should I do?"

You need a special kind of conversation: a *meta-conversation*. That's a conversation *about* conversation. Not about a specific subject, but about *how* you talk to each other (or in this case, how you *don't* talk to each other).

A: Sweetheart, I'd like to talk about something. I'd like to have a special conversation.

B: What do you mean? Are you mad?

A: No, honey. First, let me tell you what I *don't* want to talk about: sex.

B: Okay. Hey, is this a trick?

A: No, not at all. I want to talk about not talking about sex.

B: Oh, so you *do* want to talk about sex. I told you, I have nothing to say. Sometimes we do it, sometimes we don't, we more or less enjoy it, so just leave it alone.

A: Okay, okay. Look, I said I don't want to talk about sex. But I do want to talk about not talking about sex. I want to understand you better than I do. Then we'll feel closer.

B: Yeah, and I'll magically change, and become Dr. Ruth, right?

A: No. And even if you do change a little bit, that's not the point. The point is, I don't understand you as well as I want to, so I don't feel as close to you as I want to. And I can't support you as much as I want to. I promise not to try to change you. But I need to understand you better. I need that more than I need fancy sex, I'll tell you that.

B: Really?

A: Definitely.

B: So what do you want again?

A: I want to understand why you don't want to talk about sex.

B: And then what?

A: Maybe nothing. Maybe more questions. I don't know. But I promise, I won't say your reasons are stupid. At least I'll understand you better.

B: Okay. Okay. Well, I hate talking about sex. I just hate it. I've hated it for a long time. And the reason is . . . [possible reasons include I have no language, it feels dirty, it isn't ladylike, I'm too embarrassed, it will expose my ignorance, you'll laugh at me, I'm not sexy enough, etc.].

A: I see. Well, I didn't know that. Would you be willing to talk more about this feeling? There are a lot of different things we can do about it other than not talking about sex. I bet, over time, we could make some progress in helping you feel more relaxed about it. I'll do whatever I can to be helpful, without pressuring you. What I need in return is more energy coming from you to enhance our closeness.

"I'm afraid of hurting my partner's feelings. How can I suggest we try something different without him thinking I'm complaining about what we already do?"

These conversations can be difficult. Here's one way to handle a partner who is well-meaning but anxious. Notice how hostile "B" sounds, probably without intending to. Shyness, fear of being pushed, self-consciousness about being "sexy" enough, and self-criticism about being "uptight" often sound like this.

A: Hey, sometime soon, how about we do X in bed?
B: Why?
A: It might be fun.
B: Oh, you're unhappy with our sex life.
A: No, I'm actually pretty satisfied. I just want to expand things.
B: So you're unhappy.
A: No, I'd just like a little variety.
B: Because you're bored with what we do.
A: Because variety makes life richer. Like variety in food.
B: How do we know we'll like what we try?
A: We don't. It's an experiment. If we don't like it, we forget it. If we like it, we try it again when we feel like it.

B: What if one of us likes it and the other doesn't?

A: We handle it like everything else in bed: we don't do anything that both people don't like.

B: You won't resent it if I don't like something that you do?

A: No. I might be disappointed, but there're always new things to try. No need to do anything that one of us doesn't like.

B: Will these new activities mean that we stop doing things we enjoy now?

A: There's no reason to: we know that we both like them. I'd *never* give up our special stuff.

B: If you like what we already do in bed, why change now?

A: For one thing, I feel more comfortable talking about sex with you now than I used to. For another, now that we usually have pretty good sex, it makes me want to experiment more.

B: Well, I guess it wouldn't hurt to try a few new things—as long as it's only an experiment. If we do something once, it's not like we have to do it again, right?

A: Right. Exactly.

"As a guy, how can I talk about outercourse without girls thinking I'm just making excuses because I can't get it up or something?"

Yes, some women may think that about you; why not decide you don't want to be with them anyway? Most women will be pleased to have a man talk with them about sex in general, and will be really glad to have you talk about something creative and intimate like outercourse. Remember, outercourse isn't the booby prize, something you settle for.

So talk about what you *want* to talk about: the kind of connection you want, the fun and pleasure you're looking forward to, how much you're planning to please her, your hope that she'll let you know what she wants and how she feels. Don't try to control what your partner thinks about you. Pay attention, and then assume she's doing fine if she seems fine.

You always have the option of saying "Look, this isn't because I'm a wimp, or because I can't get it up. I just enjoy it/think it's a good idea/thought you might like it." When your partner soothes or reassures you, accept it graciously and let the subject go.

"When is the best time to talk about sex with my partner—on the phone before we get together, in the middle of sex, or after making love?"

Different people have different preferences in this regard. Here's the type of conversation that will help you find out what works best in any given relationship.

Have this conversation when you're feeling close. Good opportunities might include after making love, while you're cooking together, or when you're on a long drive.

A: Honey, I have a question. If I want to talk about sex, or our sex life, sometime in the future, what's the best time for us to do that?

B: What do you mean? What do you want to talk about? Is there a problem?

A: No, there's nothing I want to discuss now. That's actually the point—I wanted to get your answer to this when there wasn't something going on. I just want to know what you'd prefer—

talking about sex while we're making love, or afterward while we're cuddling, or talking about it like in the kitchen or while we're driving or whatever.

B: I don't know. What kinds of things?

A: Oh, if there's something I'd like us to try, or do differently, or if I have a question about what you like, y'know, 'That new way I kissed you last night, did you enjoy it?' I just wondered what's the best time to discuss it with you.

B: Oh. Well, for me, I guess I prefer [X]. What do you prefer?

A: Me? Um, I guess I never thought about it.

B: Well, you asked me, so now you have to answer.

A: Um, well, I guess I prefer [X or Y]. Huh, that's interesting.

B: Yeah, what you prefer is [similar to/different from] how I like to do it. I guess we'll take that into account from now on. Maybe this will make it easier for us to talk about sex after all. Thanks for bringing it up.

"Is there any way to say what I want without sounding bossy?"

Yes. In fact, If you don't feel bossy, there's a good chance you don't sound that way.

We often sound bossy when we *feel* bossy, or when we're determined to get our way. Communicating what you want, however, is a lovely gift to share with your partner. So focus on your primary goal: to communicate your desire, not to get what you want. You won't get the second without the first. Let your partner know that that's your agenda; if she misunderstands, remind her as many times as necessary: "I'm not demanding we do this, and I won't be angry if we don't. But I do want you to have the information about what I'd like."

Ask your partner if she feels bossed around, and ask if she'd prefer that you share information with her in a different way. You're not bound by her suggestions, of course, although it's to your advantage to consider what she says. If she says there isn't any way that you can ask for what you want without her feeling controlled or defensive, she's saying you shouldn't take her feelings personally. That's helpful, but still—what would you like to do about it?

For another source of information, consider how you ask for other things in ways that you feel good about (not just ways that are effective, but ways that feel good). Look at your timing, vocabulary, sensitivity, sense of confidence. Then try adapting some of those ways to sexual conversation.

"How can I get my partner to open up and talk about what he likes or wants to try?"

First, are you sure he *knows* he has an invitation to do so? This is *not* the same question as "Have you invited him?" Second, will you accept whatever he says without judgments or criticism? Third, are you already talking to him about your own desires? If not, his reticence makes perfect sense.

But let's say you can honestly answer yes to all three questions. Then, during a time when you feel close to each other, tell him how it feels not to know what he wants. Let him know how wonderful you will feel to know him better. In fact, remind him of how great it was when he communicated directly (about sex or anything else). And finally, ask how you can make it easier for him to tell you about his desires.

Encourage nonverbal communication, too: remind him he can simply move your hand a certain way or use sighs or other sounds to convey his feelings and preferences. And ask about his goals for the relationship: Does he want to get closer to you? Make the sex more satisfying or playful? How does he imagine you two will accomplish this?

Remember that ultimately, a partner's hesitation to communicate is not your responsibility. Experience him and the relationship, tell him the kind of connection (and therefore communication) you'd like, and observe his response. You can then decide what to do about things the way they are.

Chapter 9

The Future of Sex

Throughout history, the future of sex has proven notoriously difficult to predict. Looking back over time, however, there seem to be four constants about human sexual culture, which will almost certainly continue far into the twenty-first century and beyond:

1. Some percentage of people will always *experiment* with their sexual expression, exploring various forms, devising new options, and challenging cultural taboos.

This has been true throughout history: for example, group sex, homoeroticism, anal sex, dildos, contraception, consensual incest, and pornography are well-known phenomena in various cultures through time. This is true in even the most repressive cultures. The "Scarlet A" was a highly public symbol of condemnation precisely because the Puritans feared how much taboo behavior (in this case, adultery) was occurring. That's why so much cultural power was brought to bear against it.

Why do people in every culture experiment sexually? Because eroticism is a fundamental part of human nature. And, according to sociobiologists and anthropologists, the human brain is wired to desire novelty. As University of Minnesota sociologist Ira Reiss, Ph.D., reports, a look through history suggests that the more sexually repressive a culture is, the more private taboo-breaking behavior there is. One could argue, for example, that the high levels of violence and alcoholism in Ireland are an expression of pain about the notoriously intense Irish sexual repression. And the research of University of Hawaii sociologist Mickey Diamond, Ph.D., clearly shows that cultures which tightly restrict access to pornography record more sexual assault than do less porn-restrictive cultures.

2. Whatever *technologies* are invented will be *adapted* for sexual use if at all possible.

Examples in this century include the car, photography, credit cards, "900-number" phone lines, VCRs, and the Internet. In fact, sexual applications have actually driven the development and subsequent mass distribution of some fledgling technologies.

The videocassette recorder is a recent example. VCRs were a fairly expensive, exotic item until the widespread availability of inexpensive X-rated videotapes. Demand for and purchase of VCRs then took off, driving the price down, increasing the number of standard features, and making them a common household item. Other applications of VCRs (such as exercise videos, home insurance inventories, video wills, and time-delayed viewing of network programs) then followed.

Surely the discovery of how to create fire was quickly followed by someone's suggestion to make love near it, whether for warmth or for enhanced visual effect.

3. There will always be people who *react in horror* to the experimentation and adaptation described above, predicting that such behavior will undermine civilization. Such people will pressure whatever authorities they can, attempting to control others' behavior to reduce their own anxiety.

Looking over human history, these predictors of doom have never been accurate. No culture has been destroyed by sexual "excess" or experimentation. Ironically, history suggests that these same prophets of sex-negativity will continue to hinder the very things that could help prevent the terrible consequences they fear. Positive strategies for society include contraceptive availability and advertising, sex education, and promoting masturbation and outercourse for adolescents.

4. The *pendulum* of society's acceptance of sexual experimentation will continue to *swing* in both directions, creating alternating periods of sexual liberalism and repression.

All the world's great literature reflects this alternating cultural judgment. Even the Bible refers to sexual passion, bisexuality, infidelity, aphrodisiacs, and "pagan"-style sex. These clearly were not uncommon. In various times and places they were accepted, while in others they were rejected.

It is often difficult to characterize a period's sexual mood except retrospectively, and even then, there is disagreement. Examples include the fifties, early sixties, and mid-nineties: sexually repressive or relatively liberal?

Interestingly, individuals frequently make judgments about various aspects of sexuality that contrast with each other, especially these days. So, for example, a person may accept others' homosexuality but reject nonmonogamy. Or someone can forgive a mate's extramarital affair but not his/her attachment to strip clubs. A third person might see any experimentation involving intercourse as okay, but disdain oral or anal exploration. Such contrasts mirror people's complex political opinions, such as "economic conservative and civil rights liberal."

Coming Attractions

You can expect the following to be factors shaping sexual expression and experience well into the twenty-first century:

1. There will be an increasing number of *drugs* to enhance desire and sexual functioning (erection, lubrication, and orgasm). Most physicians will have neither the training nor the time to properly prepare patients to use these drugs; thus, their use will often have unintended consequences, such as new relationship pressures and conflicting new definitions of arousal and satisfaction.

CASE

Bill, Judy, and the Shots

When I first saw a busy suburban couple named the Millers, Judy had been unhappy about a lack of sex for a long time. It apparently began when her husband, Bill, developed occasional erection problems, and he started withdrawing from her sexually to avoid "failing." When he finally became frustrated enough about her complaints, he announced he was going to his doctor. "I'm going to ask for that new medicine you inject into your penis," he said, which creates erections that last for several hours.

Judy begged him not to do it. "You're missing the point," the energetic mother of three told him more than once. "Your erection isn't the most important thing. I want your caring, your sense of humor, I want to feel your total focus on us. You don't need an erection for that." But Bill went to his doctor anyway, and after a quick instructional lecture and demonstration (and no questions about how his wife felt about this), he received a prescription, which he filled on his way home.

For the next few months, whenever Bill wanted to make love he'd go into the bathroom, inject himself, and emerge saying his penis would be ready in just a few minutes (it takes the drug about twenty minutes to achieve its effect). But he didn't feel any better about himself; still preoccupied with his erection (and privately feeling that using the drug was "cheating"), he wasn't very emotionally present during sex, and so Judy still wasn't getting what she most wanted.

Her dissatisfaction confused Bill, and now he'd become angry during sex. "What do I have to do?" he'd ask. "I'm hard for three hours, what else do you want?" Despite his dependable erection, he felt like withdrawing from Judy sexually more than ever. But the short, curly-haired man wanted sex: he wanted to prove he could do it, that he could satisfy his wife, that he was still a man. So now he was pursuing sex for the wrong reason—not to enjoy it or to give pleasure, but to prove something. Judy found herself with a choice—frustrating sex or no sex. What a mess.

During several months of therapy, Judy increased her ability to describe her experience to Bill and to explain what she wanted from him in bed. Bill learned to listen better, with less defensiveness. He then realized he had some choices to make—between the performance orientation that he hoped would make him feel "like a man," and an intimacy orientation that would help him feel close to Judy and help her feel satisfied. "This is a whole different way to look at things," Bill said cautiously at one point. "I thought my pleasure, her satisfaction, and my erection were pretty much all the same. What a surprise."

Indeed, when Bill finally understood the problems he had created, his remorse was so strong it seemed as if he might disappear into it. We had to find ways for Bill to accept what he had done in order to prevent his guilt and shame .from overwhelming him and sabotaging the sex, this time from a different direction.

2. People will suffer from increasing levels of sexual *side effects* from prescription drugs, particularly as an increasing number of Americans take medications such as antidepressants and antihypertensives. Not surprisingly, people will look for an ever-

increasing amount of products, advice, and philosophy to help them cope with these side effects.

3. With life spans increasing, and baby boomers solidly encamped in middle age, part of our cultural apparatus will investigate *new models* of older sexual functioning. For example, we will see some sophisticated nursing homes offer special rooms and hours for conjugal visits (whose use will have to be approved by residents' adult children, who pay the bills). We will continue to see a higher-than-ever average age of models in magazines like *Playboy*, which already features the occasional nude woman in her forties or fifties.

4. There will be increasing cultural *pressure* to value and have "good sex," as mass advertising exploits baby boomers' anxiety about getting older and staying youthful. There will be a huge amount of products and advertising aimed at sexual dysfunction, real or imagined. Alleged aphrodisiacs, "tasteful" lingerie, and other products to set a romantic mood or enhance sexual competence will proliferate, aimed specifically at this group (marketed, no doubt, on the World Wide Web).

5. The *Internet* will be a key presence in many people's sexual lives. It will be a way of meeting potential partners, getting information about aspects of sexuality ranging from STDs to purchasing erotic products, validating non-normative preferences like cross-dressing, and participating in subcultures such as home-video swapping.

An increasing number of people will have some or all of their sex on-line—whether within a group they return to regularly, or with strangers they meet during each new encounter. Inhibited people have already found this to be the best (or only) way to experience partner sex. The Internet will provide a venue for experimenting with new sexual behaviors (such as S/M and homoeroticism) and even new sexual personae (in which people claim to be someone of a different gender, age, or race).

The varieties of virtual sex will continue to expand. A computer technology will become widely available that enables people to *feel* (not just pretend) as if they're having sexual experiences with a partner when they're actually alone. In addition, a new kind of home video-conferencing will become common: people in separate locations will be able to see and talk with each other's images while they masturbate together, describing how it feels.

6. There will be continued and increased *cultural mixing* in schools, workplaces, and entertainment, and Americans will continue to increase recreational travel to other cultures.

As a result, people will be exposed to a wider range of cultural models of sexuality, and there will be more mixed-culture couples and families. All of this points to average Americans receiving more input from "foreign" sexual and relationship models, which they will have to integrate or somehow make sense of. Some percentage will actively embrace and celebrate the opportunity to expand their sexual horizons.

7. People will continue to enter into partner sexual activity in *early adolescence*—i.e., without the psychological and communication tools they need to direct and integrate the experience. This will continue to leave a problematic residue on adults' subsequent

sexual functioning, including poor self-image, unrealistic expectations, and fear of communicating.

CASE

Karen

When Karen was growing up in rural Montana her parents meant well, but "they worked such long hours trying to make ends meet I practically never saw them," recalled the petite redhead, now a travel agent. "I started having sex really young—like fourteen—just to get some attention, y'know, just a few hugs and a word or two of approval. Well, I guess I was pretty good at pleasing guys in bed, but I didn't get much out of it. Besides," she spoke slowly, blinking back a few tears, "it didn't really work. I felt stupid, awkward. I think I knew intuitively that I still wasn't being loved for my whole self, just for the sex."

With sex such a crucial source of what little attention she received, Karen became very insecure about it. "Was I 'good enough'? I asked myself over and over," Karen said, shaking her head. "I couldn't talk to anyone, of course, being just a kid who wasn't supposed to be doing this in the first place. Besides, who could talk about sex seriously at fourteen, fifteen? I'd have died of embarrassment if anyone had looked at me and said 'vagina.' "

The insecurity followed her into adulthood and her marriage. Although she loved her husband, Jose, "I constantly feel insecure about my performance," she said. "And with all those years of putting out just to get a hug, it's hard to really see sex as something for *me*." There was another problem as well: Karen isn't comfortable with sex other than intercourse. "Jose says he likes variety," she said. "In fact, he said that sex has become pretty routine. But I guess I'm just programmed that intercourse is the most important thing to men. It certainly was to those guys when I was young."

Or at least it seemed so. Without communication skills, without the ability to talk about sex, feelings, and relationships, no one, including teenage Karen, could really ascertain what was going on in intimate situations. So that's where our therapy started—talking about what Karen wanted and felt, and exploring how to express that clearly. Transforming her simplistic, adolescent understanding of sexuality was going to take a while.

8. Social *masturbation clubs* will develop in more locations around the country. Pioneered in San Francisco and New York by gay men in the eighties, J.O. ("jack-off," slang for masturbation) clubs provide a way for people to gather for sexual activity that is medically, physically, and legally safer than cruising, barhopping, and other venues. The idea has worked so well that some cities now have clubs specifically for various sexual subgroups, such as lesbians, sadomasochists, fetishists, and yes, garden-variety heterosexuals.

J.O. clubs offer many obvious advantages to gays and others whose cruising makes them vulnerable to arrest or violence. Additionally, these clubs allow people to meet potential sex partners without having to deny their specific preferences, or pretend they're less interested in sex than they are really are. Clubs validate masturbation as a positive sexual choice, not the booby prize for losers, and they allow people to share sex without worrying about pregnancy or disease, helping to make sex truly recreational.

You can also expect to see the spread of clubs that cater to couples who want to masturbate together, spicing up their relationship with the voyeurism and exhibitionism that group activity offers.

Two Directions

As the new century rapidly approaches, sexuality appears to be heading in two different directions.

On the one hand, the full weight of American *technology* is being used to make heterosexual intercourse feasible for as many people as possible. Innovations include drugs to create erections, mechanical devices to create or maintain erections, lubricants to make intercourse more comfortable, and medical procedures that ameliorate the many reasons for painful intercourse, such as inflamed glands and endometriosis.

Each of these innovations has its advantages. In our contemporary cultural environment, however, they are not neutral or value-free. Particularly when considered as a group, these developments create additional pressure for people to want and to have intercourse. The old American spirit of "If you *can* do it you *should* do it" means that these developments sidetrack many people from adapting to their age, health, or other circumstances in ways that would otherwise naturally lead away from intercourse, toward outercourse.

This postpones the development of outercourse skills and enthusiasm, and the natural evolution of people toward a sexual persona that matches who they are becoming. It also postpones the development of our culture's acceptance of such things; in fact, this fits in with the American disposition toward denying and denigrating aging and physical limitation.

On the other hand, the last twenty years have seen an explosion of various *imaginational* modes of sexual expression: home erotica, phone sex, cybersex, inexpensive lingerie, consensual sadomasochism, sex toys, and so on.

While these are not substitutes for intercourse per se, they allow men and women to enjoy a fuller range of sexuality, focusing on imagination, exploration, sensuality, and psychological dynamics. For some people, erections and insertion are becoming less important predictors of sexual pleasure and satisfaction. As people develop this part of their erotic vocabulary, when age or health or logistics inevitably make intercourse less available or enjoyable, they have an alternative, non-intercourse model of eroticism to depend upon.

It will be interesting to see how these two directions unfold and influence each other in the future.

You, meanwhile, will always have choices—because now you can count many ways to discover great sex beyond intercourse.

Resources

* Sources for Sensual and Sexual Products

Good Vibrations
1210 Valencia St.
San Francisco, CA 94110
800/289-8423
www.goodvibes.com

Xandria Collection
Box 319005
San Francisco, CA 94131
800/242-2823
www.Xandria.com

* Sources for Sex Educational and Erotic Videotapes

Sinclair Intimacy Institute
Box 8865
Chapel Hill, NC 27515
www.bettersex.com

Focus International
1160 E. Jericho Tpke.
Huntington, NY 11743
ms@focusint.com

* To Find a Local Sex Therapist

The Society for the Scientific Study of Sexuality (SSSS)
Box 208
Mt. Vernon, IA 52314
319/895-8407
The Society@worldnet.att.com

* For Sex Education Information

Sex Information and Education Council of the United States (SIECUS)
130 W. 42 #2500
New York, NY 10036
212/819-9770

* For Information on Open and Multiple Relationships

Loving More Institute
Box 4358
Boulder, CO 80306
303/543-7540
www.lovemore.com

* For Information about Diabetes and Sexuality

www.Diabetes.com

* For Information about STDs

American Social Health Association
Box 13827
Research Triangle Park, NC 27709
919/361-8492
www.ashastd.org
National STD Hotline
800/227-8922

Bibliography

Anand, Margo: *The Art of Sexual Ecstasy* Los Angeles: Tarcher Books, 1989.

Biale, David: *Eros and the Jews* New York: Basic Books, 1992.

Foucault, Michel: *The History of Sexuality* New York: Vintage Books, 1980.

Klein, Marty: *Ask Me Anything: A Sex Therapist Answers the Most Important Questions for the '90s* Pacifica, CA: Pacifica Press, 1996.

Larue, Gerald: *Sex and the Bible* Buffalo, NY: Prometheus Books, 1983.

Lawrence, Raymond: *The Poisoning of Eros* New York: Augustine Moore Press, 1989.

Luker, Kristin: *Taking Chances* Berkeley: University of California Press, 1975.

Ramsdale, David, and Jo Ellen Dorfman: *Sexual Energy Ecstasy* Playa del Rey, CA: Peak Skill Publishing, 1985.

Reiss, Ira: *Journey into Sexuality* New York: Prentice Hall, 1986.

Robbins, Riki: *Betrayed! How to Restore Sexual Trust* Holbrook, MA, Adams Media Corporation, 1998.

Steinberg, David: *The Erotic Impulse* New York: Tarcher Books, 1992.

Tannahill, Reay: *Sex in History* New York: Stein & Day, 1980.

Zilbergeld, Bernie: *The New Male Sexuality* New York: Bantam Books, 1992.

Index

abortion, 24, 60, 129
adult-child sex, 18, 24
adultery, 49, 134, 185
advertising, 26–27, 118, 185, 189
affairs, 2, 135
affection vs. lust, 86–87
age differences, 17, 18, 23
aging, 123, 189
  sexual difficulties in, 2, 81, 135
  sexual normality and, 16, 23
  sexual satisfaction and, 121
AIDS, 45–46, 68, 121–22, 130
alcoholism, 184
ambiguity, 89–91
American Social Health Association, 197
anal sex, 27, 30, 31, 36, 45, 46, 48, 51, 55, 58, 114, 130, 183–84
  Catholics and, 108
  law and, 49–50
anger, 4, 37–39, 85, 93–94, 133, 134, 160, 187–88
anilingus, 46
anxiety, 5, 69, 92, 191–92
  about aging, 189
  about loss of erections, 65, 78
  performance vs. response, 28

anxiety (*continued*)
  about sexual normality, 8, 13–14, 21–22, 27, 28, 61, 103–4
  Viagra and, 132, 133
Apfelbaum, Bernie, 28
Aristotle, 59
arousal:
  erections vs., 133
  during sex, 113
Assyrians, 62–63
attention, paying, 65, 85, 99, 113
attitude, outercourse as, 111–13
Augustine, Saint, 41, 125

back pain, 71
Barbach, Lonnie, 10, 77
bathing, 81, 146
  together, 7, 114, 116, 149
Bedouins, 62–63
bedroom helpers, 18
bed-wetting, 82–83
"best lover" pressure, 6–7
Bible, 22–23, 40–41, 58, 185
biology vs. culture, 27–29, 43, 62–63, 75
biorhythms, 81
birth control, *see* contraception; *specific methods*—
birth control pills, 118, 129
bisexuality, 16, 36, 60, 127, 185
blaming, 76
Blanchard, Vena, 63
Blank, Joani, 26
bodily needs vs. intercourse correctly done, 81–82
Bohr, Niels, 10
boredom, 2, 15, 27–28, 85, 139, 160
Bortz, Walter, 121
breathing, 65, 146, 147–48, 161
Bull Durham (film), 114

cancer, 2
cancer treatment, 2
Caplan, Harvey, 105–6
caressing, 66, 130, 152
Catholic Church, 42, 107, 108
childbirth, recovery from, 35, 48–49
childhood abuse, 50
children:
  abandonment of, 23
  sexual behavior of, 18, 24, 37, 45
  see also teenagers
China, 62
Christianity, Christians:
  conservative, 60, 125
  sex as viewed by, 41–42, 57–59
church ritual, intercourse as, 37
Clement of Alexandria, 59
climaxing problems, 2, 13, 31, 61, 77–79, 82–83
clothing, 3, 17, 35, 46, 116
common sense, 37
communication:
  avoiding perception of bossiness in, 180–81
  best time for, 179–80
  dirty or medical words in, 165
  doctor-patient, 46–47
  without hurting partner's feelings, 177–78

improvement of, 5, 79–81, 86–87, 92–94, 115, 155, 157–58, 164–82
with insensitive partners, 173–74
nonverbal, 174–75, 181–82
with partner who refuses to talk about sex, 175–77
poor, 2, 4, 26, 69, 72, 132, 133, 134, 136, 191, 192
questions and answers about, 164–82
saying no, 172–73
spontaneity and, 165–68
with uncooperative partner, 169–71
of what you want, 2, 168–69, 174–75
community, need for, 107
condoms, 45, 61, 85, 118, 122, 129
Condylox, 47–48
connectedness, 65, 113, 128–29, 146
consent, 112
contraception, 2, 60, 71–74, 118, 123, 183–84, 185
see also specific methods—
control, 17, 75, 112
avoiding loss of, 36, 83
normality paradigm as, 16
cool vs. hot experiences, 53–54
Costner, Kevin, 114
cramps, 81
cross-dressing, 30, 60
cuddling, 115, 152
cult prostitution, 40–41, 58, 118
cultural mixing, 190
culture:
biology vs., 27–29, 43, 62–63, 75
popular, 22–27, 52–57
sexually repressive, 184
cunnilingus, 47, 50, 55, 68, 132, 153–54
cyber-sex, 119

Daily, Janet, 57
dancing, 114, 116
Denmark, 18
desire, 8, 36, 56, 119, 123, 126
incompatibilities of, 2, 13
low, 2, 84–85
during sex, 113
diabetes, 2, 120, 133, 197
Diamond, Mickey, 184
diaphragms, 73–74
dildos, 45, 183–84
disease:
sexual difficulties and, 2
see also specific diseases—
dominance and submission, 19, 100–101, 114–15
drugs, 47–48, 186–89, 193
recreational, 125
sexual difficulties and, 2, 81, 120
side effects from, 188–89
Viagra, 3, 131–36

educational system, 37
EFRAIDS (Exaggerated Fear Reaction to AIDS), 122
Egypt, ancient, 44, 118
ejaculation, 2, 34, 66–67
inhibited, 9

ejaculation (*continued*)
"premature," 20
rapid, 9, 18, 28, 68, 130
withdrawal at, 58
emotional contact, loss of, 4, 5
empowerment, of women, 26, 27
envelopment, 19, 35
environment, sexualized, 121, 165–66
erections, 5, 7, 20, 34, 64–67, 131
medication and, 2
unreliable, 2, 5, 6, 9, 15, 29, 55, 61, 64–65, 78, 98, 187
Viagra and, 3, 131–36
"erogenous zones," 112
estrus, 118
exhibitionism, 30, 115, 192
eye contact, 114, 146–47, 161, 174

fantasy, 8, 37, 116
discomfort about, 2, 22, 100–101
feeding each other, 116
fellatio, 46, 47, 55, 56, 86, 139, 165
feminists, anti-pornography, 59–60
fetishism, 46, 50
films, 52–56, 114, 164
flowers, 149–50
Focus International, 196
food and drink, 150
"foreplay," 29, 34, 35, 66
intercourse vs., 4, 85, 89, 90–91, 137–38, 153–54
fornication, 49, 58
For Yourself (Barbach), 10
Foucault, Michel, 43–45
Franz, Dennis, 55
Freudian psychology, 50
"frigidity," 45, 152–53
future of sex, 183–94
for adolescents, 190–92
aging issues and, 189
cultural mixing and, 190
drugs and, 186–89, 193
experimentation and, 183–84
horror reactions and, 185
masturbation clubs in, 192
pendulum of social acceptance and, 185–86
technology and, 184–85, 189–90, 193

Galen, 59
gas, passing, 81
genital tour, 38–39
genital warts, Condylox and, 47–48
Gnostics, 41
Good Vibrations, 26, 195
Greece, ancient, 18, 22, 125
grieving for lost opportunities, 97
group sex, 24, 37, 40
in masturbation clubs, 192
on-line, 189–90
guilt, 13, 27, 93, 188

healing intercourse-based wounds, 151–55
Heiman, Julia, 9
herpes, 68–70
Hite, Shere, 9–10
Hite Report, The (Hite), 9–10
Hittites, 62–63

HIV, 23, 121–22
homosexuality, homosexuals, 17, 20, 21, 23, 24, 45, 118, 125, 183–84
  in ancient Greece, 18
  Catholic, 108
  masturbation clubs of, 192
  prohibition of, 40
honesty, 112
horseshoes, as good luck, 10
hot vs. cool experiences, 53–54
hypertension, 120

ice, 114
identity, 29
  sexual, 8, 98
"impotence," 20, 45
incest, 24, 40, 183–84
independence:
  female, 27, 60
  from normality paradigm, 16
Industrial Age, 118
infidelity, 49, 134, 185
initiation, sexual, 18
intercourse, 33–87
  bodily needs vs., 81–82
  complaints about what is required for, 62–74
  complaints about what it's supposed to be like, 62, 74–87
  complete and "normal," 34–35
  cult of, 34
  disease and, 2
  evolution of, 117–19
  "foreplay" vs., 4, 85, 89, 90–91, 137–38, 153–54
  gender and, 44
  as generic sex, 53–54
  healing wounds from, 151–55
  language of, 19, 29, 53
  law and, 49–50
  medical emphasis on, 44–49
  moderation and, 35–36
  orgasm and, 10, 13, 28, 77–79, 130–31, 153–54
  outercourse combined with, 159–61
  painful, 2, 38, 83–85, 120
  preference for, 30
  psychological emphasis on, 50–52
  reproduction and, 40–43, 57, 161–63
  rushing of, 4, 5, 6
  in Tantra, 129
intercourse, deemphasizing of, 5, 6, 10, 87–108
  ambiguity in, 89–91
  challenges created by, 89–97
  communication in, 92–94
  creating what you want in, 106–7
  "just sex" and, 101–3
  knowing what you want from sex in, 105–6
  meaningful stories in, 107–8, 125–26
  obsolete categories in, 95–96
  opportunities created by, 97–103
  questioning other things in, 95
  recertification ended by, 98–99
  safer introspection in, 99–100
  self-validation in, 107, 124–25

intercourse, deemphasizing of (*continued*)
and "sexuality" in broad terms, 105
staying present with yourself in, 91–92
toleration of partner in, 100–101
intercourse conspiracy, 59–60
intercourse sabbatical, 139, 155–58, 160–61
variations on, 157–58
Internet, 189–90
intimacy, 5, 7, 28, 37, 42, 50, 114, 119, 136, 146, 187–88
introspection, safer, 99–100
Inuit, language of, 19
Ireland, 17, 184
isolation, decreasing sense of, 14

Japan, 18, 63
Jerome, 41
Jews, Judaism, 18, 57
dietary laws of, 40
pikuach nefesh in, 70–71
sexual behavior of, 40–41, 44, 63
J.O. ("jack-off") clubs, 192
Johnson, Susan, 56
Johnson, Virginia, 9
Journey into Sexuality (Reiss), 42–43
"just sex," 101–3

Kahun Papyrus, 44
kinship, 42
kissing, 54, 66, 114, 130, 132, 135, 147, 150, 152

Landers, Ann, 37, 46
language, 18–22, 29, 165
Larue, Gerald, 58
law, 49–50, 118
Lawrence, Raymond, 41, 58
Lawrence Research Group, 26
Leiblum, Sandra, 9
long-term relationships, desire for satisfaction in, 121
LoPiccolo, Joseph, 9
lotion, playing with, 115
lousy sex, loss of interest in, 3–4
love, 36, 56, 107, 146
Loving More Institute, 197
lubrication, 85
anal sex and, 114
artificial, 38, 39, 62, 63, 81, 150, 193
natural, 2, 5, 62
Luker, Kristin, 72
lust, 123
vs. affection, 86–87

McLuhan, Marshall, 53
Macomber, Debbie, 56–57
Madonna, 55
magazines:
sex, 26, 189
S/M, 60
women's, 26–27, 37
Maimonides, 44
Male Sexuality (Zilbergeld), 9
manual stimulation, 7, 13, 30, 31, 50, 86, 95, 131
marriage, 42, 57–58
massage, 115
Masters, William, 9

masturbation, 6, 22, 24, 45, 47, 58, 114, 151
  future of, 185, 190, 192
  by married people, 13, 31
  mutual, 23, 55, 114, 132
masturbation clubs, 192
meaningful stories, telling yourself, 107–8, 125–26
media, sex and, 7–8, 14, 25, 36, 52–56, 118
medical institutions, 118, 135
  sexual normality and, 14, 44–49
meditation, 146
menstruation, 18, 63
meta-conversation, 175–77
Middle Ages, 18, 44, 118
moderation, 35–36
money, sex for, 16, 17
monogamy, 118
mothers, new, 48–49
Ms., 26–27
MTV, 54–55
music, 146, 149

Navajo, language of, 18–19
nipple stimulation, 86, 115
"no," saying, 2, 172–73
normality paradigm, *see* sexual normality
novels, romance, 56–57
nudity, 24, 189
NYPD Blue (TV show), 55

oil, playing with, 115
old categories, obsolescence of, 95–96
oral sex, 13, 19, 30, 45, 46, 48, 51, 114, 130, 131, 135
  law and, 49–50
  in romance novels, 56–57
  see also anilingus; cunnilingus; fellatio
orgasms, 2, 5, 20
  faking of, 37
  fear of bed-wetting and, 82–83
  female, 10, 28, 31, 35, 37, 67, 82–83, 130, 131, 154–55
  intercourse and, 10, 13, 28, 77–79, 130–31, 153–54
  through manual stimulation, 7, 13, 30, 31, 95
  outercourse and, 130–31
  simultaneous, 78
osteoporosis, 2
outercourse (non-intercourse sex), 109–82
  activities in, 114–16
  advantages of, 119–31
  breathing in, 147–48
  communication in, 155, 164–82
  defined, 111–13
  details of, 127–31
  as genderless, 44
  healing intercourse-based wounds in, 151–55
  inclusiveness of, 130
  intercourse combined with, 159–61
  intercourse sabbatical in, 139, 155–58
  in mass media, 52–56
  as non-normal sex, 124–26
  presence and, 141–44, 161

outercourse (non-intercourse sex) (*continued*)
sensuality in, 148–51
spirituality and trance in, 144–47
Tantra compared with, 129
for variety, 50
see also intercourse, deemphasizing of; *specific types of outercourse*—

Pacific cultures, 18
pain, 9, 17, 46, 120
of being "abnormal," 27
chronic, 2, 70–71, 81, 120
during intercourse, 2, 38, 83–85, 120
passion, 18, 37, 39, 56, 185
Paul, Saint, 58
pedophilia, 23
pelvic muscles, strengthening of, 82
penetration, 19, 34, 35
penis, 65–66
importance placed on, 19
in partner vs. solo sex, 6
see also ejaculation; erections
performance pressure, 4–7, 9, 28–29, 64, 131, 154
performance vs. presence, 141–44
phone sex, 115
pikuach nefesh, 70–71
Playboy, 26, 189
playfulness, 20, 28, 113
Poisoning of Eros, The (Lawrence), 41
political activism, 16
politicians, antichoice, 59–60
polygamy, 24, 118
popular culture, 22–27, 52–57
advertising and, 26–27
MTV in, 54–55
NYPD Blue in, 55–56
romance novels in, 56–57
pornography, 24, 59–60, 116, 183–84
Posner, Richard, 49
preferences, 8, 30–31, 35, 99–100, 126, 192
discomfort about, 2
pregnancy, 72, 73–74, 129–30
teenage, 23, 55, 122
presence, 91–92, 141–44, 161
pre-teens, 60
prostitution, 16, 17, 36, 60
cult, 40–41, 58, 118
psychiatry, sexual normality and, 14, 17, 36, 50–52
psychology, sexual normality and, 50–52
Puritans, 184

questioning other things, 95
quieting the mind, 146

Rajneesh, 125
recertification, end of need for, 98–99
refractory period, 66–67
Reiss, Ira, 42–43, 44, 184
religion, 118
sexual normality and, 13, 14, 37, 40–42, 57–60
see also Christianity, Christians; Jews, Judaism
reproduction, intercourse and, 40–43, 57, 161–63

resources, 106–7, 195–97
response anxiety, 28
responsibility, 112, 143
role-playing, 35, 48
romance novels, 56–57
Romans, ancient, 22
Russia, 18, 63

sadomasochism (S and M), 19, 30, 46, 60, 125, 127
safe sex, 45, 121–22
Schnarch, David, 16, 93
self-criticism, 92, 147, 160
self-exploration and expression, 120, 124–26, 128, 193–94
self-fulfillment, 27, 31
self-help, self-help books, 3, 37
self-image, 88
self-validation, 107, 124–25
semen, magical qualities seen in, 58–59
senses, use of, 143, 148–51
sensual and sexual products, sources for, 195
"sex addiction," 3, 13, 50
sex education, 60, 185
  information sources for, 196
Sex Information and Education Council of the United States (SIECUS), 196
sex-reassignment surgery, 119
sex therapists, finding, 196
sexual difficulties, 1–9
  sexual normality and, 8, 14
  shame about, 8, 10
  see also specific problems—
sexual experience vs. sexual normality, 8, 14–15
sexual identity, 8, 98
sexually transmitted diseases (STDs), 23, 45–46
  AIDS, 45–46, 68, 121–22, 130
  herpes, 68–70
  information sources for, 197
sexual normality, 2, 13–87
  anxiety about, 8, 13–14, 21–22, 27, 28, 61, 103–4
  creation of, 36–37
  escaping from, 103–5
  expansion of definition of, 16–17
  how people relate to, 27–29
  language and, 18–22, 29
  popular culture and, 22–27
  relief from pressure of, 16–17
  sexual experience vs., 8, 14–15
  social forces in construction of, 43–59
  variations in definition of, 17–18
sexual positions, 34, 81
  peaceful, 70
sexual relating, need for new forms of, 122–23
sexual values, clash of, 60
shame, 188
  sexual difficulties and, 8, 10
  about sexually transmissible conditions, 69
  sexual normality and, 17, 27
Shaw, George Bernard, 165
showering, *see* bathing
sibling-sibling sex, 24
Sinclair Institute, 196

sixty-nine, 31
"slut," 19, 102
Snead, Louise, 57
Society for the Scientific Study of Sexuality, The (SSSS), 196
sodomy laws, 49–50
spirituality, sex and, 18, 36, 42, 62, 113, 123, 144–47
spontaneity, 79–81, 165–68
staying present with yourself, 91–92
stereotypes, sexual, 25
strip clubs, 60
stripping, 116
"stud," 19
subcultures, sexual, 60, 125
surgery, 35, 119

Taking Chances (Luker), 72
Tannahill, Reay, 59
Tantra, 129
technology, sex and, 184–85, 189–90, 193
teenagers, 23, 55, 122, 123, 185
  contraception for, 60
  future of sex for, 190–92
teeth, brushing of, 81
television, 52–56, 114, 164
  daytime talk shows on, 7–8
textures, playing with, 115, 149
thrusting, 34, 70, 85
toys, sex, 46, 60
trance, 144–47

United States, as sex-obsessed society, 7–8
urination, 81, 82–83

vaginal infections, 68, 69
vaginal lubrication, 2, 5
vaginal soreness, 28
Viagra, 3, 131–36
vibrators, 26, 45, 115
Victorian England, 20, 62
videocassette recorders (VCRs), 184–85
videotapes:
  making of, 116
  sources for, 196
  X-rated, 59–60, 184
violence, 24, 184, 192
voyeurism, 30, 116, 192

warts, genital, Condylox and, 47–48
water, 114
whispering, 150
wife-swappers, 36
Winfrey, Oprah, 37
"womanizer," 19

Xandria Collection, 195
X-rated videos, 59–60, 184

Zilbergeld, Bernie, 9

About the Authors

Dr. Marty Klein has been a Licensed Marriage and Family Counselor and Sex Therapist for nineteen years. His articles regularly appear in publications such as *New Woman, Playboy,* and the *Journal of Sex Research.* He was recently honored by both the California Association of Marriage & Family Therapists and the Society for the Scientific Study of Sexuality. His website address is: www.SexEd.org

Riki Robbins, nationally known relationship expert, holds a Ph.D. from Harvard and a certificate in Clinical Sexology from the Institute for Advanced Study of Human Sexuality. She is the author of three books: *The Empowered Woman, Negotiating Love,* and *Betrayed: How to Restore Sexual Trust.* Dr. Robbins has conducted hundreds of seminars nationwide and now consults in Berkeley, California. Her website is: www.askdrriki.com